IRISH LOVE POEMS

Dánta Grá

Edited by:
Paula J. Redes
Illustrations by:
Peadar Mc Daid
Introduction By:
Gabriel Rosenstock

Hippocrene Books
New York
Roberts Books
Dublin

This book is dedicated to the many
individuals whose words and
inspirations have allowed it to be.

Copyright © 1996 by Hippocrene Books, Inc.

Second printing, 1997.

All rights reseved.

For information, address:
HIPPOCRENE BOOKS, INC.
171 Madison Avenue
New York, NY 10016

Distributed in Ireland by Roberts Wholesale Books, Limited,
Unit 12, Benson Street Enterprise Centre, Hanover Quay, Dublin 2

Library of Congress Cataloging-in-Publication-Data
Irish love poems / edited by Paula J. Redes
p.   cm.
Includes bibliographical references and index.
ISBN 0-7818-0396-9
1. Love poetry, English—Irish authors.   2.   Man-woman
relationships—Ireland—Poetry.   I. Redes, Paula J.
PR8861.L6I75   1996
821.008'0354—dc20   95-49337
                                                            CIP
Printed in the United States of America

CONTENTS

Acknowledgments

The editor gratefully acknowledges the permission of writers and publishers to reprint the following copyright material:

Sara Berkeley: for "The Parting" reprinted from *Penn* (Thistledown Press Ltd., 1992).

Austin Clarke: for "Mable Kelly" reprinted from *Flight to Africa* by kind permission of the estate of Austin Clarke.

John Deane: for "Sacrament" reprinted from Winter *in Meath* by kind permission of Dedalus Press.

Nuala Ní Dhomhnaill: for "Labasheedy" reprinted from *Selected Poems* with permission of New Island Books.

Paul Durcan: for "An Ancient Wireless" reprinted from *The Selected Paul Durcan* (Thistledown Press Ltd, 1989).

Gabriel Fitzmaurice: for "Garden" from *Rainsong* and "In The Midst Of Possibility" from *Dancing Through* reprinted by kind permission of the author. Translations of "Entanglement," "Vietnam Love Song," and "Entreaty" by Caitlín Maude are reprinted from *An Crann faoi Bhlath/The Flowering Tree* by kind permission of the translator.

Seamus Heaney: for "A New Song" from *Poems 1965-1975* (1980). Reprinted by permission of Farrar, Straus & Giroux, Inc.

Fred Johnston: for "For Emma" and "We Are Rivers, Frozen" reprinted from *Song at the End of the World* with permission of Salmon Publishing, Galway.

Brendan Kennelly: for "Bread" reprinted from *A Time for Voices* (Bloodaxe Books, 1990) by permission of Bloodaxe Books Ltd.

Medbh McGuckian: for "On Not Being Your Lover " from *The Flower Master and Other Poems* (1994) and "The Sofa" from *Venus and the Rain* (1994) reprinted by kind permission of the author and The Gallery Press.

Tom Mac Intyre: for "Killen Hill" reprinted from *I Bailed out at Ardee* by kind permission of Dedalus Press.

John Montague: for "Pastorals" reprinted from *Collected Poems* (1995) by kind permission of the author and The Gallery Press. "All Legendary Obstacles" reprinted from *Selected Poems* (1995) with permission of Wake

Forest University Press.

Paul Muldoon: for "Something of a Departure" reprinted from *Why Brownlee Left* by permission of Wake Forest University Press.

Desmond O'Grady: for "In The Greenwood" reprinted from *A Limerick Rake* (1973) by kind permission of the author and The Gallery Press.

Mary O'Malley: for "Aftermath" reprinted from *A Consideration of Silk* with permission of Salmon Publishing, Galway.

Gabriel Rosenstock: for "The Search" reprinted from *An Crann faoi Bhlath/The Flowering Tree* by kind permission of the author.

James Simmons: for "The End Of The Affair" reprinted from *Poems 1956-1986* (1986) by kind permission of the author and The Gallery Press. "A Long Way After Ronsard" reprinted by kind permission of the author.

Jo Slade: for "When Our Heads Bend" reprinted from *In Fields I Hear Them Sing* with permission of Salmon Publishing, Galway.

Introduction

A Personal Perspective
by Gabriel Rosenstock

"A pity beyond all telling is hid in the heart of love. . ." So wrote Yeats. And yet poets from earliest times have told us what is hidden, have sung their joy and sorrow, the exuberance and the mystery of love.

Long ago in Ireland, a poet once invited the object of his affections to enter another realm in his company:

> *A ainnir fionn an raghfá liom*
> *Go tír na n-iontas, tír an cheoil. . .*

> (Fair lady will you come with me
> To the land of wonders, the land of music. . .)

No fanciful dreaming this—on his part or our own. The belief in another world is much more than the sublimation of grief, personal or tribal; it's more than a transcendence of all that flesh is heir to. It is, in Castaneda's words, an initiation into 'a separate reality'. Language and song can only hint at that, but they point to it so eloquently that we are left with little doubt that vision poetry has its origins in a realm beyond the ordinary laws of physics, of supply and demand, and all the other material and civic laws that seek to define our existence. The power of poetry, coupled with the power of love, is a force to be reckoned with. Both are alive and well and living in Ireland.

The ethereality of the native Irish poetic genius is equally matched by earthy, concrete realism. Here is my translation into English of one of the hundreds of exquisite Irish love poems and love songs from the native corpus, *Ná Tar ach San Oíche:*

If You Come

If you come at all
Come only at night,
Tread ever so warily
And please don't scare me.
Under the door
You'll find the key
And I'll be alone—
Don't frighten me!

No pot is in your way
Not a stool or a can
Or a rope of hay
Not a pin, man!
The dog is so tame
He won't bat an eye—
And where's the shame,
I trained him, didn't I?

Mother's asleep,
Dad's hands on her hips,
Kissing her mouth,
Her slow-opening lips.
Ah now, it's fine for her!
But my heart is lead—
Lying on my own
In a feathery bed.

Many of the poets represented in this most welcome anthology—**Thomas Moore**, let us say, infinitely more popular in the drawing rooms of London's comfortable classes than in the length and breadth of Ireland—would find the above traditional poem slightly indelicate. But Ireland, Gaelic Ireland in particular, was immune to many of the "civilizing" forces of Europe, the Renaissance, the Reformation, the Enlightenment, the *isms* of art and literature, absorbing and Gaelicizing Scandinavian and Norman influences in turn, untouched by Victorian Puritanism until the English tide, with the cooperation of the clergy, finally flooded a broken land with middle-class aspirations towards respectability and cultural assimilation.

The old spirit was not entirely quenched and an anonymous poet was not afraid to sing:

Níl fhios a'm 'bhfuil peaca na drúise
Chomh trom 'bhíonns na sagairt á rá

(I don't know if the sin of lust
Is as mortal as the priests do say!)

Chesterton may not have exaggerated when he said:

The great Gaels of Ireland,
The men whom God made mad,
For all their wars are merry
And all their songs are sad!

To hear that ineffable, keening sadness one should listen to Máire Áine Ní

Dhonnchadha singing *Úna Bhán* in the recording *Deora Aille* (Claddagh Records). Terrifying, magical, heart-rending! Another such love-lament, now very rarely sung, if at all, has the lines:

> *Tráthnóna aréir bhí an spéir go sámh, gan scamall scáth ná smúit,*
> *Ach beadsa féin i m'aonarán ó cailleadh Máire Bhúis!*

The poet laments the death of one Mary Bushe, killed by a bull! The cultured aesthete recoils at this, saying it is not a fit subject for poetry. But a bull was the hero of our national epic, the *Táin*. Yeats himself, then a Senator, was responsible for commissioning the design of a new Irish coinage and to this day a bull adorns the five-penny piece. The bull, therefore, may not seem as "poetical" as the nightingale or the swan, but in pre-Christian Ireland divination was practiced at the *tarbhfheis*, or bull-feast, at which the flesh of the bull was ceremoniously consumed. The crowning irony is that the word "bull" is used to describe the ludicrousness of Irish speech, at a time when the Irish had only recently mastered English—"his brother and sister are much alike, especially his sister." Certain Irish writers and entertainers consciously played this up, polishing a certain quixotry or quaintness of language and the reader may best judge, from examples in this anthology, where the device is conscious or not.

In the love-song, *A Ógánaigh Óig*, the strength of the poet's love is described thus:

> *Is gur daingne a bhí mise i do ghrása*
> *Ná mar bhíonns na tairní i gcruth na n-each. . .*

> (And my love for you was even stronger
> Than the sturdy nails of a horse's shoe. . .)

Ethereality, materiality, fused in artistry!

As Irish began to decline, after the Great Famine of the mid-nineteenth century, there was a profusion of macoronic songs—Irish alternating with English. A County Limerick bachelor sang like this:

> *D'imíos féinig go dtí an agent*
> *To know if he'd take me mar chliamhain isteach;*
> *Ach uair orm ann a ghlaoigh sé in a terrible rage now*
> *Agus mura mbeadh mabhstar Éasar I would be shot!*

(I went to the agent, To know if he'd take me as a son-in-law; And once there he was in a terrible rage now, And were it not for Meister Äser, I would be shot!)

The macoronic confusion is compounded by the presence of a Paletine;

these were Germans who settled in County Limerick following religious persecution at home. To this day, *Iníon an Phalaitínigh* (**The Paletine's Daughter**) is a popular love-song.

It was Douglas Hyde's translations of Connaught love-songs that engendered the frisson between the old culture and the new and sparked off the Irish Literary Renaissance. The poem by **Yeats**, *The Ragged Wood* (pg. 77), says, "O my share of the world". This is literally from the Irish idiom: *a chuid den tsaol.*

Dublin, too, it must be said, has its own peculiar sensibilité, wit, and lingo:

> But there was a fly in the ointment
> Which you very seldom see,
> For though I loved her terrible well
> She was in love with a Portugue!
> (*The Maid from Cabra West*)

Though he wrote in English, **Samuel Lover** (pg. 32) exudes the Gaelic spirit:

> What will you do, Love, when I am going
> With white sails flowing, the seas beyond. . .

The internal rhyme throughout the poem—going/flowing—is typical of Gaelic artistry.

Love is extended here to encompass love of country, as in Mangan's rousing version of *Róisín Dubh*, **Dark Rosaleen** (pg. 35). In this poem, Ireland is personified as a woman, a typical device of the *aisling* or vision poem of Jacobite times. (We shouldn't forget that Ireland owes her name, **Éire**, to a goddess—*Éiriú.*)

There are quite a few poems and ballads in this anthology from Paula Redes which, I fear, need to be sung to be believed! This would seem to be true of **Kitty of Coleraine** (pg 41), **Slievnamon** (pg. 41), **The Spinning Wheel Song** (pg. 43), **Down by the Sally Gardens** (pg. 74), and the Thomas Moore medleys (pgs. 23 - 28) in particular.

Let me conclude by echoing a Gaelic poet,

> *"Aobhinn, a leabhráin, do thriall!"*
> ("Beautiful, oh book, thy journey!")

GABRIEL ROSENSTOCK
DUBLIN

IRISH
LOVE
POEMS

Anonymous

Eily Mavourneen
(From the Lily of Killarney)

Eily Mavourneen, I see thee before me,
Fairer than ever, with Death's pallid hue
Mortal thou art not, I humbly adore thee,
Yea with a love which thou knowest is true.
Look'st thou in anger ah! no, such a feeling
Ne'er in thy too gentle heart had a place,
Softly the smile of forgiveness is stealing,
Eily my own, o'er thy beautiful face.

Once would my heart with the wildest emotion
Throb, dearest Eily, when near me wert thou,
Now I regard thee with deep, calm devotion,
Never, bright angel, I lov'd thee as now.
Though in this world were so cruelly blighted
All the fond hopes of thy innocent heart,
Soon in a holier region united,
Eily Mavourneen, we never shall part,
Soon in a holier region united,
Eily Mavourneen, we never shall part,
Soon in a holier region united,
Eily Mavourneen, we never shall part.

I Know Where I'm Going

I know where I'm goin';
And I know who's goin' with me,
I know who I love,
But the dear knows who I'll marry!

I have stockings of silk,
Shoes of fine green leather,
Combs to buckle my hair,
And a ring for every finger.

I have treasures of gold,
In my heart all hidden;
Only my grief untold,
And a trembling tear unbidden.

Feather beds are soft,
And painted rooms are bonny,
But I would leave them all
To go with my love Johnny.

Strangers pass me by
In this world I'm lonely,
For my Johnny I sigh,
For 'tis him that I love only.

Some say he is dark
But I say he's bonny,
The bravest of them all
My handsome winning Johnny.

I know where I'm goin'
And I know who's goin' with me,
I know who I love,
But the dear knows who I'll marry!

Nahum Tate

The Penance

Nymph fanaret, the gentlest maid
That ever happy swain obeyed,
(For what offense I cannot say)
A day and night, and half a day,
Banished her shepherd from her sight:
His fault for certain was not slight,
Or sure this tender judge had ne'er
Imposed a penance so severe.
And lest she should anon revoke
What in her warmer rage she spoke,
She bound the sentence with an oath,
Protested by her Faith and Troth,
Nought should compound for his offense
But the full time of abstinence.
Yet when his penance-glass were run,
His hours of castigation done,
Should he defer one moment's space
To come and be restored to grace,
With sparkling threat'ning eyes she swore
That failing would incense her more
Than all his trespasses before.

George Farquhar

"Thus Damon Knock'd At Celia's Door"

Thus Damon knock'd at Celia's Door,
Thus Damon knock'd at Celia's Door,
He sigh'd and begg'd and wept and swore,
The sign was so, She answer'd no,
The sign was so, She answer'd no, no, no no.

Again he sigh'd, again he pray'd,
No, Damon, no, no, no, no, no, I am afraid;
Consider, Damon, I'm a Maid,
Consider, Damon, no, no, no, no, no, no, no,
    I'm a Maid.

At last his Sighs and Tears made way,
She rose and softly turn'd the key;
Come in, said she, but do not, do not stay,
I may conclude, you will be rude;
But if you are you may:
I may conclude, you will be rude,
But if you are you may.

Oliver Goldsmith

When Lovely Woman

When lovely woman stoops to folly,
And finds too late that men betray;
What charm can soothe her melancholy
What art can wash her guilt away?

The only art her guilt to cover,
To hide her shame from every eye,
To give repentance to her lover,
And wring his bosom, is—to die.

Richard Brinsley Sheridan

The Geranium

In the close covert of a grove,
By nature formed for scenes of love,
Said Susan, in a lucky hour,
Observe yon sweet geranium flower;
How straight upon its stalk it stands,
And tempts our violating hands:
Whilst the soft bud as yet unspread,
Hangs down its pale declining head:
Yet, soon as it is ripe to blow,
The stems shall rise, the head shall glow.
Nature, said I, my lovely Sue,
To all her followers lends a clue;
Her simple laws themselves explain,
As links of one continued chain;
For her the mysteries of creation,
Are but the works of generation:
Yon blushing, strong, triumphant flower,
Is in the crisis of its power:
But short, alas! its vigourous reign,
He sheds his seed, and drops again;

The bud that hangs in pale decay,
Feels not, as yet, the plastic ray;
To-morrow's sun shall bid him rise,
Then, too, he sheds his seed and dies:
But words, my love, are vain and weak,
For proof, let bright example speak;
Then straight before the wondering maid,
The tree of life I gently laid;
Observe, sweet Sire, his drooping head,
How pale, how languid, and how dead;
Yet, let the sun of thy bright eyes,
Shine but a moment, it shall rise;
Let but the dew of thy soft hand
Refresh the stem, it straight shall stand:
Already, see, it swells, it grows,
Its head is redder than the rose,
Its shrivelled fruit, of dusky hue,
Now glows, a present fit for Sue:

21

The balm of life each artery fills,
And in o'erflowing drops distills.
Oh me! cried Susan, when is this?
What strange tumultuous throbs of bliss!
Sure, never mortal, till this hour,
Felt such emotion as a flower:
Oh, serpent! cunning to decieve,
Sure, 'tis this tree that tempted Eve;

The crimson apples hang so fair,
Alas! what woman could forbear?
Well, hast thou guessed, my love, I cried,
It is the tree by which she died;
The tree which could content her,
All nature, Susan, seeks the center;
Yet, let us still, poor Eve forgive,
It's the tree by which we live;
For lovely woman still it grows
And in the centre only blows.
But chief for thee, it spreads its charms,
For paradise is in thy arms. —
I ceased, for nature kindly here
Began to whisper in her ear:
And lovely Sue, lay softly panting,
While the geranium tree was planting.
'Till in the heat of amorous strife,
She burst the mellow tree of life.
"Oh Heaven!" cried Susan, with a sigh,
"The hour we taste, —we surely die;
Strange raptures seize my fainting frame,
And all my body glows with flame,
Yet let me snatch one parting kiss
To tell my love I die with bliss:
That pleased, thy Susan yields her breath;
Oh! who would live if this be death!"

Thomas Moore

"At The Mid Hour Of Night..."

At the mid hour of night, when stars are weeping, I fly
To the lone vale we loved, when life shone warm in thine
    eye;
    And I think oft, if spirits can steal from the regions of
      air
    To revisit past scenes of delight, thou wilt come to me
      there,
And tell me our love is remembered even in the sky.

Then I sing the wild song it once was rapture to hear,
When our voices commingling breathed like one on the
    ear;
    And as Echo far off through the vale my sad orison
      rolls,
    I think, O my love! 'tis thy voice from the Kingdom of
    Souls
Faintly answering still the notes that once were so dear.

Love's Young Dream

    The days are gone, when beauty bright
      My heart's chain wove;
    When my dream of life, from morn till night,
      Was love, still love.

    New hope may bloom,
    And days may come,
Of milder, calmer beam;
But there's nothing half so sweet in life
    As love's young dream.

Did Not

(FROM JUVENILE POEMS, 1801)

'Twas a new feeling—something more
Than we had dared to own before,
   Which then we hid not:
We saw it in each other's eye,
And wished, in every half-breathed sigh,
To speak, but did not.

She felt my lips impassioned touch—
'Twas the first time I dared so much,
   And yet she chid not;
But whispered o'er my burning brow,
"Oh, do you doubt I love you now,"
Sweet Soul! I did not.

Warmly I felt her bosom thrill,
I prest it closer, closer still,
Though gently bid not,
   Till—oh! the world hath seldom heard
   Of lovers, who so nearly erred,
And yet, who did not.

Though Lost To Sight To Memory Dear

Sweetheart, goodbye! That flut'ring sail
Is spread to waft me far from thee;
   And soon, before the farthr'ing gale
My ship shall bound upon the sea.
   Perchance, all des'late and forlorn,
These eyes shall miss thee many a year;
   But unforgotten every charm—
Though lost to sight, to memory dear.

   Sweetheart, goodbye! one last embrace!
Oh, cruel fate, two souls to sever!
   Yet in this heart's most sacred place
Thou, thou alone, shalt dwell forever;
   And still shall recollection trace,
In fancy's mirror, ever near,
   Each smile, each tear, that form, that face—
Though lost to sight, to memory dear.

The Irish Peasant To His Mistress

Through grief and through danger thy smile hath cheer'd my way,
Till hope seem'd to bud from each thorn that round me lay;
The darker our fortune, the brighter our pure love burn'd,
Till shame into glory, till fear into zeal was turn'd:
Yes, slave as I was, in thy arms my spirit felt free,
And bless'd even the sorrows that made me more dear to thee.

Thy rival was honour'd while thou wert wrong'd and scorn'd;
Thy crown was of briars, while gold her brows adorn'd;
She woo'd me to temples, whilst thou lay'st hid in caves;
Her friends were all masters, while thine, alas! were slaves;
Yet cold in the earth, at thy feet, I would rather be
Than wed what I loved not, or turn one thought from thee.

They slander thee sorely, who say thy vows are frail—
Hadst thou been a false one, thy cheek had look'd less pale!
They say, too, so long thou hast worn those lingering chains,
That deep in thy heart they have printed their servile stains:
O, foul is the slander! —no chain could that soul subdue—
Where shineth thy spirit, there Liberty shineth too!

Believe Me, If All Those Endearing Young Charms

Believe me, if all those endearing young charms,
    Which I gaze on so fondly to-day,
Were to change by to-morrow, and fleet in my arms,
    Like fairy-gifts fading away!

Thou wouldst still be adored, as this moment thou art,
    Let thy loveliness fade as it will,
And around the dear ruin each wish of my heart,
    Would entwine itself verdantly still.

It is not while beauty and youth are thine own,
    And thy cheeks unprofaned by a tear,
That the fervor and faith of a soul may be known,
    To which time will but make thee more dear!
O the heart that has truly loved never forgets,
    But as truly loves on to the close,
As the sunflower turns to her god when he sets
    The same look which she turned when he rose!

Black And Blue Eyes

The brilliant black eye
    May in triumph let fly
All its darts without caring who feels 'em;
    But the soft eye of blue,
    Though it scatter wounds too,
Is much better pleased when it heals 'em!
    Dear Fanny!

The black eye may say,
    "Come and worship my ray;
By adoring, perhaps you may move me!"
    But the blue eye, half hid,
    Says, from under its lid,
"I love, and am yours, if you love me!"
    Dear Fanny!

Then tell me, O why,
    In that lovely blue eye,
Not a charm of its tint I discover;

Or why should you wear
The only blue pair
That ever said "No" to a lover!
Dear Fanny!

Mary, I Believed Thee True

Mary, I believed thee true,
  And I was blest in thus believing:
But now I mourn that e'er I knew
  A girl so fair and so deceiving.
Few have ever loved like me;
  O, I have loved thee too sincerely:
And few have e'er deceived like thee,
  Alas! deceived me too severely.
      Fare thee well!

Fare thee well! yet think awhile
  On one whose bosom seems to doubt thee;
Who now would rather trust that smile,
  And die with thee than live without thee.
Fare thee well! I'll think on thee.
  Thou leav'st me many a bitter token;
For see, distracting woman, see
  My peace is gone, my heart is broken.
      Fare thee well!

Charles Wolfe

To Mary

If I had thought thou couldst have died,
  I might not weep for thee;
But I forgot, when by thy side,
  That thou couldst mortal be:
It never through my mind had past
  The time would e'er be o'er,
And I on thee should look my last,
  And thou shouldst smile no more!

And still upon that face I look,
  And think 'twill smile again;
And still the thought I will not brook,
  That I must look in vain.
But when I speak—thou dost not say
  What thou ne'er left'st unsaid;
And now I feel, as well I may,
  Sweet Mary, thou art dead!

If thou wouldst stay, e'en as thou art,
  All cold and all serene—
I still might press thy silent heart,
  And where thy smiles have been.

While e'en thy chill, bleak course I have,
  Thou seemest still mine own;
But there—I lay thee in the grave,
  And now I am alone.

I do not think, where'er thou art,
  Thou hast forgotten me;
And I, perhaps, may soothe this heart
  In thinking too of thee:
Yet there was round thee such a dawn
  Of light ne'er seen before,
As fancy never could have drawn,
  And never can restore!

William Maginn

Waiting For The Grapes

That I love thee, charming maid, I a thousand times have said,
 And a thousand times more I have sworn it,
But 't is easy to be seen in the coldness of your mein
 That you doubt my affection—or scorn it.
Ah me!

Not a single grain of sense in the whole of these pretenses
 For rejecting your lover's petitions;
Had I windows in my bosom, O how gladly I'd expose 'em!
 To undo your fantastic suspicions
Ah me!

You repeat I've known you long, and you hint I do you wrong,
 In beginning so late to pursue ye;
But 't is folly to look glum because people did not come
 Up the stairs of your nursery to woo ye.
Ah me!

In a grapery one walks without looking at the stalks,
 While the bunches are green that they're bearing:
All the pretty little leaves that are dangling at the eaves
 Scarce attract e'en a moment of staring.
Ah me!

But when time has swelled the grapes to a richer style of shapes,
 And the sun has lent warmth to their blushes,
Then to cheer us and to gladden, to enchant us and to madden,
 Is the ripe rudy glory that rushes.
Ah me!

O, 't is then that mortals pant while they gaze on Bacchus plant, —
 O, 't is then, —will my simile serve ye?
Should a damsel fair repine, though neglected like a vine?
 Both erelong shall turn heads topsy-turvey.
Ah me!

Samuel Lover

Rory O'More;
(OR, ALL FOR GOOD LUCK)

Young Rory O'More courted Kathleen bawn—
He was bold as a hawk, she as soft as the dawn;
He wished in his heart pretty Kathleen to please,
And he thought the best way to do that was to tease.
"Now Rory, be aisy!" sweet Kathleen would cry,
Reproof on her lips, but a smile in her eye—
"With your tricks, I don't know, in troth, what I'm about;
Faith! you've tazed me till I've put on my cloak inside out."
"Och! jewel," says Rory, "That same is the way
Ye've thrated my heart for this many a day;
And 'tis plazed that I am, and why not, to be sure?
For 'tis all for good luck," says bold Rory O'More.

"Indeed, then," says Kathleen, "don't think of the like,
For I half gave a promise to soothering Mike:
The ground that I walk on he loves, I'll be bound—"
"Faith," says Rory, "I'd rather love you than the ground."
"Now, Rory, I'll cry if you don't let me go;
Sure I dream every night that I'm hating you so!"
"Och," says Rory, that same I'm delighted to hear,
For dhrames always go by conthraries, my dear.
So, jewel, keep dhraming that same till ye die,
And bright morning will give dirty night the black lie!
And 'tis plazed that I am, and why not, to be sure!
Since 'tis all for good luck," says bold Rory O'More.

"Arrah, Kathleen, my darlint, you've tazed me enough;
Sure I've thrashed, for your sake, Dinny Grimes and Jim Duff;
And I've made myself, drinking your health, quite a baste—
So I think, after that, I may talk to the praste."
Then Rory, the rogue, stole his arm round her neck,
So soft and so white, without freckle or speck;
And he looked in her eyes, that were beaming with light,
And he kissed her sweet lips—don't you think he was right?
"Now, Rory, leave off, sir—you'll hug me no more—
That's eight times to day that you've kissed me before."
"Then here goes another," says he, "to make sure!
For there's luck in odd numbers," says Rory O'More.

What Will You Do, Love?

"What will you do, love, when I am going,
With white sail flowing, the seas beyond,
What will you do, love, when waves divide us,
And friends may chide us for being fond?"
"Tho' waves divide us, and friends be chiding,
In faith abiding, I'll still be true,
And I'll pray for thee on the stormy ocean
In deep devotion—that's what I'll do."

"What would you do, love, if distant tidings,
Thy fond confidings should undermine;
And I, abiding 'neath sultry skies
Should think other eyes were as bright as thine?"
"Oh! name it not! tho' guilt and shame
Were on thy name, I'd still be true!
But that heart of thine, should another share it,
I could not bear it—what would I do?"

"What would you do, love, when home returning,
With hopes high burning, with wealth for you,
If my barque which bounded o'er foreign foam,
Should be lost near home—ah! what would you do?"
"So thou wert spar'd, I'd bless the morrow,
In want and sorrow, that left me you!
And I'd welcome thee from the wasting billow,
This heart thy pillow—that's what I'd do."

Gerald Griffen

Song

A place in thy memory, dearest,
　　Is all that I claim,
To pause and look back when thou hearest
　　The sound of my name.
Another may woo thee nearer,
Another may win and wear;
I care not, though he be dearer,
If I am remembered there.

Could I be thy true lover, dearest,
　　Couldst thou smile on me,
I would be the fondest and nearest
　　That ever loved thee.
But a cloud o'er my pathway is glooming
Which never must break upon thine,
And Heaven, which made thee all blooming,
Ne'er made thee to wither on mine.

Remember me not as a lover
　　Whose fond hopes are crossed,
Whose bosom can never recover
　　The light it has lost;
As the young bride remembers the mother,
She loves, yet never may see,
As a sister remembers a brother,
Oh, dearest, remember me.

James Clarence Mangan

Dark Rosaleen

O my dark Rosaleen,
    Do not sigh, do not weep!
The priests are on the ocean green,
    They march along the deep.
There's wine from the royal Pope,
    Upon the ocean green;
And Spanish ale shall give you hope,
    My dark Rosaleen!
    My own Rosaleen!
Shall glad your heart, shall give you hope,
Shall give you health and help, and hope,
    My Dark Rosaleen.

Over hills, and through dales,
    Have I roamed for your sake;
All yesterday I sailed with sails
    On river and on lake.
The Erne, at its highest flood,
    I dashed across unseen,
For there was lightning in my blood,
    My dark Rosaleen!
    My own Rosaleen!
Oh! there was lightning in my blood,
Red lightning, lightened through my blood,
    My Dark Rosaleen!

All day long in unrest,
    To and fro do I move,
The very soul within my breast
    Is wasted for you, love!
The heart in my bosom faints
    To think of you, my Queen,
My life of life, my saint of saints,
    My dark Rosaleen!

My own Rosaleen!
To hear your sweet and sad complaints,
My life, my love, my saint of saints,
  My Dark Rosaleen!

Woe and pain, pain and woe,
  Are my lot, night and noon,
To see your bright face clouded so,
  Like to the mournful moon.
But yet will I rear your throne
  Again in golden sheen;
'Tis you shall reign, shall reign alone,
  My dark Rosaleen!
  My own Rosaleen!
'Tis you shall have the golden throne,
'Tis you shall reign, shall reign alone,
  My Dark Rosaleen!

 Over dews, over sands,
  Will I fly for your weal:
Your holy, delicate white hands
  Shall girdle me with steel.
At home in your emerald bowers,
  From morning's dawn to e'en,
You'll pray for me, my flower of flowers,
  My dark Rosaleen!
  My fond Rosaleen!
You'll think of me your daylight's hours,
My virgin flower, my flower of flowers,
  My Dark Rosaleen!

I could scale the blue air,
  I could plow the high hills,
Oh, I could kneel all night in prayer,
  To heal your many ills!
And one beamy smile from you
  Would float like light between
My toils and me, my own, my true,

My dark Rosaleen!
My fond Rosaleen!
Would give me life and soul anew,
A second life, a soul anew,
　My Dark Rosaleen!

O! the Erne shall run red
　With redundance of blood,
The earth shall rock beneath our tread,
　And flames wrap hill and wood,
And gun-peal, and slogan cry

　Wake many a glen serene,
Ere you shall fade, ere you shall die,
　My dark Rosaleen!
　My own Rosaleen!
The Judgment Hour must first be nigh
Ere you can fade, ere you can die,
　My Dark Rosaleen!

Helen Lady Selina Dufferin

Lament Of The Irish Immigrant

I'm sittin' on the stile, Mary,
 Where we sat side by side
On a bright May mornin' long ago,
 When first you were my bride;
The corn was springin' fresh and green,
 And the lark sang loud and high—
And the red was on your lip, Mary,
 And the love-light in your eye.

The place is little changed, Mary,
 The day is bright as then,
The lark's loud song is in my ear,
 And the corn is green again;
But I miss the soft clasp of your hand,
 And your breath warm on my cheek,
And I still keep list'ning for the words
 You never more will speak.

'Tis but a step down yonder lane,
 And the little church stands near,
The church where we were wed, Mary,
 I see the spire from here.
But the graveyard lies between, Mary,
 And my step might break your rest—
For I've laid you darling! down to sleep,
 With your baby on your breast.

I'm very lonely now, Mary,
 For the poor make no new friends,
But, O, they love the better still,
 The few our Father sends!
And you were all I had, Mary,
 My blessin' and my pride:
There's nothin' left to care for now,
 Since my poor Mary died.

Yours was the good, brave heart, Mary,
 That still kept hoping on,
When the trust in God had left my soul,
 and my arm's young strength was gone:

There was comfort ever on your lip,
    And the kind look on your brow—
I bless you, Mary, for that same,
    Though you cannot hear me now.

I thank you for the patient smile
    When your heart was fit to break,
When the hunger pain was gnawin' there,
    And you hid it, for my sake!
I bless you for the pleasant word,
    When your heart was sad and sore—
O, I'm thankful you are gone, Mary,
    Where grief can't reach you more!

I'm biddin' you a long farewell,
    My Mary—kind and true!
But I'll not forget you, darling!
    In the land I'm goin' to;
They say there's bread and work for all,
    And the sun shines always there—
But I'll not forget old Ireland,
    Were it fifty times as fair!

And often in those grand old woods
    I'll sit and shut my eyes,
And my heart will travel back again
    To the place where Mary lies;
And I'll think I see a little stile
    Where we sat side by side:
And the springin' corn, and the bright May morn,
    When first you were my bride.

Katey's Letter

Och, girls dear, did you ever hear I wrote my love a letter?
And although he cannot read, sure, I thought 'twas all the better
For why should he be puzzled with hard spelling in the matter,
When the meaning was so plain that I loved him faithfully?
I love him faithfully—
And he knows it, oh, he knows it, without one word from me.

I wrote it, and I folded it and put a seal upon it;
'Twas a seal almost as big as the crown of my best bonnet—
For I would not have the postmaster make his remarks upon it,
As I said inside the letter that I loved him faithfully,
I love him faithfully—
And he knows it, oh, he knows it without one word from me.

My heart was full, but when I wrote I dare not put the half in;
The neighbors know I love him, and they're mighty fond of chaffing,
So I dared not write his name outside for fear they would be laughing,
So I wrote "From little Kate to one whom she loves faithfully."
I love him faithfully—
And he knows it, oh, he knows it, without one word from me.

Now, girls, would you believe it, that postman's so consated,
No answer will he bring me so long as I have waited—
But maybe there may not be one for the reason that I stated,
That my love can neither read nor write, but he loves me faithfully,
He loves me faithfully—
And I know where'er my love is that he is true to me.

Charles Dawson Shanley

Kitty Of Coleraine

As beautiful Kitty one morning was tripping
    With a pitcher of milk, from the fair of Coleraine,
When she saw me she stumbled, the pitcher it tumbled,
    And all the sweet buttermilk watered the plain.
"O, what shall I do now? —'t was looking at you now!
    Sure, sure such a pitcher I'll ne'er meet again!
'T was the pride of my dairy: O Barney M'Cleary!
    You're sent as a plague to the girls of Coleraine."

I sat down beside her, and gently did chide her,
    That such a misfortune should give her such pain.
A kiss then I gave her; and ere did I leave her,
    She vowed for such pleasure she'd break it again.

'T was hay-making season—I can't tell the reason—
    Misfortunes will never come single, 't is plain;
For very soon after poor Kitty's disaster
    The devil a pitcher was whole in Coleraine.

John Francis Waller

The Spinning-Wheel Song

Mellow the moonlight to shine is beginning;
Close by the window young Eileen is spinning;
Bent o'er the fire, her blind grandmother, sitting,
Is croaning, and moaning, and drowsily knitting,—
"Eileen, a chora, I hear someone tapping."
" 'T is the ivy, dear mother, against the glass flapping."
"Eileen, I surely hear somebody sighing."
" 'T is the sound, mother dear, of the summer wind dying."

Merrily, cheerily, noisily whirring,
Swings the wheel, spins the wheel, while the foot's stirring;
Sprightly, and lightly, and airily ringing,
Thrills the sweet voice of the young maiden singing.

"What's that noise that I hear at the window, I wonder?"
" 'T is the little birds chirping the holly-bush under."
"What makes you be shoving and moving your stool on,
And singing all wrong that old song of 'The Coolun' ?"
There's a form at the casement, the form of her true-love,
And he whispers, with face bent, "I'm waiting for you, love;
Get up on the stool, through the lattice step lightly,
We'll rove in the grove while the moon's shining brightly."

Merrily, cheerily, noisily whirring,
Swings the wheel, spins the reel, while the foot's stirring;
Sprightly, and lightly, and airily ringing,
Thrills the sweet voice of the young maiden singing.

The maid shakes her head, on her lip lays her fingers,
Steals up from her seat, —longs to go, and yet lingers;
A frightened glance turns to her drowsy grandmother,
Puts one foot on the stool, spins the wheel with the other.
Lazily, easily, swings now the wheel round;
Slowly and lowly is heard now the reel's sound;
Noiseless and light to the lattice above her
The maid steps,—then leaps to the arms of her lover.

Slower—and slower—and slower the wheel swings;
Lower—and lower—and lower the reel rings;
Ere the reel and the wheel stop their ringing and moving,
Through the grove the young lovers by moonlight are roving.

Patrick Hogan

A Shawl Of Galway Grey

'Twas short the night we parted,
Too quickly came the day,
When silent, broken-hearted,
I went from you away,
The dawn was brightening o'er Glenrue
As stole the stars away,
The last fond look I caught of you
An' your shawl of Galway Grey.

Oh, I've seen the silks and laces—
An' well they look and show—
Beneath the pretty faces
Of gentle girls I know,
But this—a secret I'll confide—
I'd leave them all to-day
To meet you on a green hillside
In your shawl of Galway Grey.

The well is sparkling as of yore,
The sky still grey and blue,
The dog outside your father's door
Keeps watch and ward for you;
An' all this picture now I see—
But, ah! so far away—
Is bright'ned by your grace so free
An' your shawl of Galway Grey.

Let others love some prouder dame
With frills and flowers bedecked,
Your power o'er me is still the same,
Its play remains unchecked.
An' all I wish for is Glenrue,
My homeland far away,
An' life an' love beside you
In your shawl of Galway Grey.

Sir Samuel Ferguson

Cashel of Munster
(From the Irish)

I'd wed you without herds, without money or rich array,
   And I'd wed you on a dewy morn at day-dawn gray;
My bitter woe it is, love, that we are not far away
In Cashel town, tho' the bare deal board were our marriage-bed
   this day!

O fair maid, remember the green hill-side,
   Remember how I hunted about the valleys wide;
Time now has worn me, my locks are turn'd to gray;
The year is scarce and I am poor—but send me not, love, away!

O deem not my blood is of base strain, my girl;
   O think not my birth was as the birth of a churl;
Marry me and prove me, and say soon, you will
That noble blood is written on my right side still.

My purse holds no red gold, no coin of the silver white;
   No herds are mine to drive through the long twilight;
But the pretty girl that would take me, all bare tho' I be and 'lone,
O, I'd take her with me kindly to the county Tyrone!

O my girl, I can see 'tis in trouble you are;
And O my girl, I see 'tis your people's reproach you bear!
—I am a girl in trouble for his sake with whom I fly,
And, O, may no other maiden know such reproach as I.

Cean Dubh Deelish

Put your head darling, darling, darling,
Your darling black head my heart above;
   O mouth of honey, with thyme for fragrance,
Who, with heart in breast, could deny you love?

O many and many a young girl for me is pining,
Letting her locks of gold to the cold wind free,
   For me, the foremost of our gay young fellows;
But I'd leave a hundred, pure love, for thee.

Then put your head, darling, darling, darling,
Your darling black head my heart above;
   O mouth of honey, with thyme for fragrance,
Who, with heart in breast, could deny you love?

Aubrey De Vere

Her Shadow

Bending between me and the taper,
  While o'er the harp her white hands strayed,
The shadows of her waving tresses
  Above my hand were gently swayed.
With every graceful movement waving,
  I marked their undulating swell;
I watched them while they met and parted,
  Curled close or widened, rose or fell.

I laughed in triumph and in pleasure—
  So strange the sport, so undesigned!
Her mother turned and asked me, gravely,
  "What thought was passing through my mind ?"

'T is Love that blinds the eyes of mothers;
  'T is Love that makes the young maids fair!
She touched my hand; my rings she counted;
  Yet never felt the shadows there.

Keep, gamesome Love, beloved Infant,
  Keep ever thus all mothers blind;
And make thy dedicated virgins,
  In substance as in shadow, kind!

Sir Charles Gavan Duffy

The Patriot's Wife

Oh! give me back that royal dream
    My fancy wrought,
When I have seen your sunny eyes
    Grow moist with thought;
And fondly hoped, dear love, your heart from mine
    Its spell had caught;
And laid me down to dream that dream divine,
    But true, methought,
Of how my life's long task would be, to make yours
    blessed as it ought.

To learn to love sweet nature more
    For your sweet sake,
To watch with you—dear friend, with you!—
    Its wonders break;
The sparkling spring in that bright face to see
    Its mirrors make—
On summer morns to hear the sweet birds sing
    By linn and lake;
And know your voice, your magic voice, could still a
    grander music wake!
To wake the old weird world that sleeps
    In Irish lore;
The strains sweet foreign Spenser sung
    By Mulla's shore;
Dear Curran's airy thoughts, like purple birds
    That shine and soar;
Tone's fiery hopes, and all the deathless vows
    That Gratten swore;
The songs that once our own dear Davis sung—ah me!
    to sing no more.

And all those proud old-victor fields
    We thrill to name,
Whose memories are the stars that light
    Long nights of shame;
The Cairn, The Dan, The Rath, The Power, The Keep,
    That still proclaim
In chronicles of clay and stone, how true, how deep

Was Éire's fame;
Oh! we shall see them all, with her, that dear, dear friend
we two have loved the same.

Yet ah! how truer, tenderer still
　　　Methought did seem
That scene of tranquil joy, that happy home
　　　By Dodder's stream.
The morning smile, that grew a fixéd star
　　　With love-lit beam,
The ringing laugh, locked hands, and all the far
　　　And shining stream
Of daily love, that made our daily life diviner than a
　　dream.

For still to me, dear friend, dear love,
　　　Or both—dear wife,
Your image comes with serious thoughts,
　　　But tender, rife;
No idle plaything to caress or chide
　　　In sport or strife,
But my best chosen friend, companion, guide,
　　　To walk through life,
Linked hand-in-hand, two equal, loving friends, true
　　husband and true wife.

Denis Florence MacCarthy

Love And Time

Two pilgrims from the distant plain
    Come quickly o'er the mossy ground.
One is a boy, with locks of gold
    Thick curling round his face so fair;
The other pilgrim, stern and old,
    Has snowy beard and silver hair.

The youth with many a merry trick
    Goes singing on his careless way;
His old companion walks as quick,
    But speaks no word by night or day.
Where'er the old man treads, the grass
    Fast fadeth with a certain doom;
But where the beauteous boy doth pass
    Unnumbered flowers are seen to bloom.

And thus before the sage, the boy
    Trips lightly o'er the blooming lands,
And proudly bears a pretty toy—
    A crystal glass with diamond sands.
A smile o'er any brow would pass
    To see him frolic in the sun—
To see him shake the crystal glass,
    And make the sands more quickly run.

And now they leap the streamlet o'er
    A silver thread so white and thin,
And now they reach the open door,
    And now they lightly enter in:
"God, save all here" —that kind wish flies
    Still sweeter from his lips so sweet;
"God, save you kindly," Norah cries,
    "Sit down, my child, and rest and eat."

"Thanks, gentle Norah, fair and good,
    We'll rest awhile our weary feet;
But though this old man needeth food,
    There's nothing here that he can eat.
His taste is strange, he eats alone,

Beneath some ruined cloister's cope,
Or on some tottering turret's stone,
   While I can only live on—hope!

"A week ago, ere you were wed—
   It was the very night before—
Upon so many sweets I fed
   While passing by your mother's door—
It was that dear, delicious hour
   When Owen here the nosegay brought,
And found you in the woodbine bower—
   Since then, indeed, I've needed naught."

A blush steals over Norah's face,
   A smile comes over Owen's brow,
A tranquil joy illumines the place,
   As if the moon were shining now;
The boy beholds the pleasing pain,
   The sweetest confusion he has done,
And shakes the crystal glass again,
   And makes the sands more quickly run.

"Dear Norah, we are pilgrims, bound
   Upon an endless path sublime;
We pace the green earth round and round,
   And mortals call us LOVE and TIME;
He seeks the many, I the few;
   I dwell with peasants, he with kings.
We seldom meet; but when we do,
   I take his glass; and he my wings."

"And thus together on we go,
   Where'er I chance or wish to lead;
And time, whose lonely steps are slow,
   Now sweeps along with lightening speed.
Now on our bright predestined way
   We must to other regions pass;
But take this gift, and night and day
   Look well upon its truthful glass."

"How quick or slow the bright sands fall
   Is hid from lovers' eyes alone,
If you can see them move at all,
   Be sure your heart has colder grown.

'Tis coldness makes the glass grow dry,
    The icy hand, the freezing brow;
But warm the heart and breathe the sigh,
    And then they'll pass you know not how."

She took the glass where love's warm hands
    A bright impervious vapor cast,
She looks, but cannot see the sands,
    Although she feels they're falling fast.
But cold hours came, and then, alas!
    She saw them falling frozen through
Till love's warm light suffused the glass,
    And hid the loosening sands from view!

William Allingham

Lovely Mary Donnelly

O lovely Mary Donnelly, it's you I love the best!
If fifty girls were around you, I'd hardly see the rest;
Be what it may the time of day, the place be where it will,
Sweet looks of Mary Donnelly, they bloom before me still.

Her eyes like mountain water that's flowing on a rock,
How clear they are! how dark they are! and they give me many
  a shock;
Red rowans warm in sunshine, and wetted with a shower,
Could ne'er express the charming lip that has me in its power.

Her nose is straight and handsome, her eyebrows lifted up,
Her chin is very neat and pert, and smooth like a china cup;
Her hair's the brag of Ireland, so weighty and so fine, —
It's rolling down upon her neck, and gathered in a twine.

The dance o' last Whit-Monday night exceeded all before;
No pretty girl for miles around was missing from the floor;
But Mary kept the belt of love, and O, but she was gay;
She danced a jig, she sung a song, and took my heart away!

When she stood up for dancing, her steps were so complete,
The music nearly killed itself, to listen to her feet;
The fiddler mourned his blindness, he heard her so much
  praised,
But blessed himself he wasn't deaf when once her voice she
  raised.

And evermore I'm whistling or lilting what you sung;
Your smile is always in my heart, your name beside my tongue.
But you've as many sweethearts as you'd count on both your
  hands,
And for myself there's not a thumb or little finger stands.
O, you're the flower of womankind, in county or in town;
The higher I exalt you, the lower I'm cast down.
If some great lord should come this way and see your beauty
  bright,
And you to be his lady, I'd own it was but right.

O, might we live together in lofty palace hall,
Where joyful music rises, and where scarlet curtains fall;
O, might we live together in a cottage mean and small,
With sods of grass the only roof, and mud the only wall!

O lovely Mary Donnelly, your beauty's my distress;
It's far too beauteous to be mine, but I'll never wish it less;
The proudest place would fit your face, and I am poor and low,
But blessings be about you, dear, wherever you may go!

Charles J. Kickham

Slievenamon

Alone, all alone, by the wave-wash'd strand,
And alone in the crowded hall.
The hall it is gay, and the waves they are grand,
But my heart is not here at all!
It flies far away, by night and by day,
To the time and the joys that are gone!
And I never can forget the sweet maiden I met,
In the Valley near Slievenamon.

It was not the grace of her queenly air,
Nor her cheek of the rose's glow,
Nor her soft black eyes, nor her flowing hair,
Nor was it her lily-white brow.
'Twas the soul of truth and of melting ruth,
And the smile like a summer dawn,
That stole my heart away one soft summer day,
In the Valley near Slievenamon.

In the festive hall, by the star-watch'd shore,
Ever my restless spirit cries:
'My love, oh, my love, shall I ne'er see you more?
And, my land, will you never uprise?
By night and by day, I ever, ever, pray,
While lonely my life flows on,
To see our flag unrolled, and my true love to enfold,
In the Valley near Slievenamon.

Charles G. Halpine

Quakerdom
(The Formal Call)

Through her forced, abnormal quiet
Flashed the soul of frolic riot,
And a most malicious laughter lighted up her downcast
eyes;
All in vain I tried each topic,
Ranged from polar climes to tropic, —
Every commonplace I started met with yes-or-no replies.

For her mother—stiff and stately,
As if starched and ironed lately—
Sat erect, with rigid elbows bedded thus in curving palms;
There she sat on guard before us,
And in words precise, decorous,
And most calm, reviewed the weather, and recited several
psalms.

How without abruptly ending
This my visit, and offending
Wealthy neighbors, was the problem which employed my
mental care;
When the butler, bowing lowly,
Uttered clearly, stiffly, slowly,
"Madam, please, the gardener wants you," —
Heaven, I thought, has heard my prayer.

"Pardon me!" she grandly uttered;
Bowing low I gladly muttered,
"Surely, madam," and, relieved, I turned to scan the
daughter's face:
Ha! what pent-up mirth outflashes
From beneath those penciled lashes!
How the drill of Quaker custom yields to Nature's
brilliant grace.

Brightly springs the prisoned fountain
From the side of Delphis mountain

When the stone that weighed upon its buoyant life is
    thrust aside;
        So the long-enforced stagnation
        Of the maiden's conversation
Now imparted five-fold brilliance to its ever-varying tide.

        Widely ranging, quickly changing,
        Witty, winning, from beginning
Unto end I listened, merely flinging in a casual word:
        Eloquent, and yet how simple!
        Hand and eye, and eddying dimple,
Tongue and lip together made a music seen as well as
    heard.

        When the noonday woods are ringing,
        All the birds of summer singing,
Suddenly there falls a silence, and we know a serpent
    nigh:
        So upon the door a rattle
        Stopped our animated tattle,
And the stately mother found us prim enough to suit her
    eye.

John Boyle O'Reilly

A White Rose

The red rose whispers of passion,
    And the white rose breathes of love;
O, the red rose is a falcon,
    And the white rose is a dove.

But I send you a cream-white rosebud
    With a flush upon its petal tips;
For the love that is purest and sweetest
    Has a kiss of desire on the lips.

J.M. Crofts

Could I But Hear

Could I but hear thy voice that charmeth,
Him who lends a grateful ear,
Whisp'ring soft the heart alarmeth,
To a trembling silent tear,
Sweet maiden dear to me that greeting,
Tender sweet for ever more,
In vain shall I await thy meeting,
Till for us life's dream be o'er.

Ah! dearest one, if thou couldst love me,
Broken-hearted tho' I be,
Bright as silv'ry stars above thee,
Realms of lore I built for thee!
Though passing time my dreams shall sever,
Love is greater far than fame,
In life in death I'm thine for ever,
This relic mine shall be thy name.

Isabella Valancy Crawford

We Parted In Silence

We parted in silence, we parted by night,
 On the banks of that lonely river;
Where the fragrant limes their boughs unite,
 We met—and we parted forever!
The night-bird sung, and the stars above
 Told many a touching story,
Of friends long passed to the kingdom of love,
Where the soul wears its mantle of glory.

We parted in silence,— our cheeks were wet
 With the tears that were past controlling;
We vowed we would never, no, never forget,
 And those vows at the time were consoling;
But those lips that echoed the sounds of mine
 Are as cold as that lonely river;
And that eye, that beautiful spirit's shrine,
 Has shrouded its fires forever.

And now on the midnight sky I look,
 And my heart grows full of weeping;
Each star is to me a sealéd book,
 Some tale of that loved one keeping.
We parted in silence,—we parted in tears,
 On the banks of that lonely river:
But the odor and bloom of those bygone years
 Shall hang o'er its waters forever.

George Moore

Sonnet
(From Flowers of Passion, 1878)

I am most lovely, fair beyond desire:
My breasts are sweet, my hair is soft and bright,
And every movement flows by instinct right:
Full well I know my touch doth burn like fire,
That my voice stings the sense like smitten lyre;
I am the queen of sensuous delight;
Past years are sealed with the signet of my might;
And at my feet pale present kneels a buyer.

My beds are odorous with soft-shed scent,
And strange moon flowers a tremulous twilight air
Weave over all; and here, alone I sing
My siren songs, until all souls are bent
Within the subtle sweet melodious snare.
God, making love, made me love's grievous sting.

Rondo
(From Flowers of Passion, 1878)

Did I love thee? I only did desire
To hold thy body unto mine,
And smite it with strange fire
Of kisses burning as a wine,
And catch thy odorous hair, and twine
It thro' my fingers amorously.
        Did I love thee?

 Did I love thee? I only did desire
To watch thine eyelids lilywise
Closed down, and thy warm breath respire
As it came through the thickening sighs;
And seek my love in such fair guise
Of passions' sobbing agony.
        Did I love thee?

Did I love thee? I only did desire
To drink the perfume of thy blood
In vision, and thy senses tire
Seeing them shift from ebb to flood
In consonant sweet interlude,
And if love such a thing not be,
    I loved not thee.

The Triumph Of The Flesh
(From Pagan Poems, 1881)

We have passed from the regions of dreams and of visions
And the flesh is the flesh and the rose is the rose;
And we see but the absolute joy of the present
    In the Sunlight of beauty.

I am filled with carnivorous lust: like a tiger
I crouch and I feed on my beautiful prey:
There is nought in the monstrous world of Astarte
    So fair as thy body.

Let me lie, let me die on thy snow-covered bosom,
I would eat of thy flesh as of delicate fruit,
I am drunk of its smell, and the scent of thy tresses
    Is as flame that devours.

Thou art demon and God, thou art Hell, thou art Heaven,
Thou art love that is lust, thou art lust that is love,
And I see but the heavenly grace of thy body,
    A picture—a poem.

And the flesh is a soul tho' it be art eternal.

William Drummond

Madrigal

Like the Idalian queen,
Her hair about her eyne,
With neck and breasts ripe apples to be seen,
    At first-glance of the morn
In Cyprus' gardens gathering those fair flow'rs
    Which of her blood were born.
I saw, but fainting saw, my paramours.
The graces naked danced about the place,
    The winds and trees amazed
    With silence on her gazed,
The flowers did smile, like those upon her face;
And as their aspen stalks those fingers band,
    That she might read my case,
A hyacinth I wish'd me in her hand.

Her Passing

The beauty and the life
    Of life's and beauty's fairest paragon
    —O tears! O grief!—hung at a feeble thread
To which pale Atropos had set her knife;
    The soul with many a groan
    Had left each outward part,
And now did take his last leave of the heart:
Naught else did want, save death, ev'n to be dead;
When the afflicted band about her bed,
Seeing so fair him come in lips, cheeks, eyes,
Cried, 'Ah! and can Death enter Paradise!?'

William Cox Bennett

The Worn Wedding-Ring

Your wedding-ring wears thin, dear wife; ah, summers
    not a few,
Since I put it on your finger first, have passed o'er me and
    you;
And, love, what changes we have seen,—what cares and
    pleasures, too,—
Since you became my own dear wife, when this old ring
    was new!

O, blessings on that happy day, the happiest of my life,
When, thanks to God, your low, sweet "Yes" made you
    my loving wife!
Your heart will say the same, I know; that day's as dear to
    you,—
That day that made me yours, dear wife, when this old ring
    was new.

How well do I remember now your young sweet face that
    day!
How fair you were, how dear you were, my tongue could
    hardly say;
Nor how I doted on you; O, how proud I was of you!
But did I love you more than now, when this old ring was
    new?

No—no! no fairer were you then that at this hour to me;
And, dear as life to me this day, how could you dearer be?
As sweet your face might be that day as now it is, 'tis true;
But did I know your heart as well when this old ring was
    new?

O partner of my gladness, wife, what care, what grief is
    there
For me you would not bravely face, with me you would
    not share?
O, what a weary want had every day, if wanting you,
Wanting the love that God made mine when this old ring
    was new!

Years bring fresh links to bind us, wife,— young voices
    that are here;
Young faces round our fire that make our mother's yet more
    dear;
Young loving hearts your care each day makes yet more
    like to you,
More like the loving heart made mine when this old ring
    was new.

And blessed be God! all he has given are with us yet; around
Our table every precious life lent to us still is found.
Though cares we've known, with hopeful hearts the worst
    we've struggled through;
Blessed be his name for all his love since this old ring was
    new!

The past is dear, its sweetness still our memories treasure
    yet;
The griefs we've borne, together borne, we would not now
    forget.
Whatever, wife, the future brings, heart unto heart still
    true,
We'll share as we have shared all else since this old ring
    was new.

And if God spare us 'mongst our sons and daughters to
    grow old,
We know his goodness will not let your heart or mine grow
    cold.
Your agéd eyes will see in mine all they've still shown to
    you,
And mine in yours all they have seen since this old ring
    was new.

And O, when death shall come at last to bid me to my rest,
May I die looking in those eyes, and resting on that breast;
O, may my parting gaze be blessed with the dear sight of
    you,
Of those fond eyes,— fond as they were when this old ring was
    new!

Katherine Tynan

Any Wife

Nobody knows but you and I, my dear,
And the stars, the spies of God, that lean and peer,
Those nights when you and I in a narrow strait
Were under the whips of God and desolate.
In extreme pain, in uttermost agony,
We bore the cross for each other, you and I,
When, through the darkest hour, the night of dread,
I suffered and you supported my head.

Ties that bind us together for life and death,
O hard-set fight in the darkness, shuddering breath,
Because a man can only bear as he may,
And find no tears for easing, the woman's way,
Anguish of pity, sharp in the heart like a sword;
Dost Thou not know, O Lord? Thou knowest, Lord,
What we endured for each other: our wounds were red
When he suffered and I supported his head.

Grief that binds us closer than smile or kiss,
Into the pang God slips the exquisite bliss.
You were my angel and I your angel, as he,
The angel, comforted Christ in His agony,
Lifting Him up from the earth that His blood made wet,
Pillowing the Holy Head, dabbled in sweat,
Thou who wert under the scourges knowest to prove
Love by its pangs, love that endures for love.

The Return

I rested in your easy chair,
   Slept in your late-abandoned bed
And felt your pleasure everywhere,
   A benediction on my head,
Through sleep and waking: all the while
I was quite sure I felt your smile.

I knelt and laid my cheek upon
   The cushions that you lately pressed;
All your familiar things forgone
   Took to my own use and behest,
Quite sure your spirit leant to bless
Your daughter in that loneliness.

I sat beside your fire aglow,
   In the dim hours 'twixt night and day,
And knew you would be glad to know,
   You who gave everything away—
I had your old room, sweet and warm,
Safe from the winter night and storm.

I slept, I rose, I rested there;
   My thoughts, my dreams were still and glad.
The dear room kept its happy air
   As in the golden years we had;
And sleeping, waking, all the while
I was quite sure I felt your smile.

William Butler Yeats

The Lover Mourns For The Loss Of Love

Pale brows, still hands and dim hair,
I had a beautiful friend
And dreamed that the old despair
Would end in love in the end:
She looked in my heart one day
And saw your image was there;
She has gone weeping away.

O Do Not Love Too Long

Sweetheart, do not love too long:
I loved long and long,
And grew to be out of fashion
Like an old song.

All through the years of our youth
Neither could have known
Their own thought from the other's
We were so much at one.

But O, in a minute she changed—
O do not love too long,
Or it will grow out of fashion
Like an old song.

Down By The Sally Gardens

Down by the sally gardens,
My love and I did meet;
She passed the sally gardens,
With little snow-white feet,
She bid me take love easy,
As the leaves grow on the tree,
But I was young and foolish,
With her did not agree.

In a field by the river,
My love and I did stand;
And on my leaning shoulder,
She laid her snow-white hand.
She bid me take love easy,
As the grass grows on the weirs;
But I was young and foolish,
And now am full of tears.

No Second Troy

Why should I blame her that she filled my days
With misery, or that she would of late
Have taught to ignorant men most violent ways,
Or hurled the little streets upon the great,
Had they but courage equal to desire?
What could have made her peaceful with a mind
That nobleness made simple as a fire,
With beauty like a tightened bow, a kind
That is not natural in an age like this,
Being high and solitary and most stern?
Why, what could she have done, being what she is?
    Was there another Troy for her to burn?

Ephemera

'Your eyes that once were never weary of mine
Are bowed in sorrow under pendulous lids,
Because our love is waning.'

And then she:
'Although our love is waning, let us stand
By the lone border of the lake once more,
Together in that hour of gentleness
When the poor child, Passion, falls asleep,
How far away the stars seem, and how far
Is our first kiss, and ah, how old my heart!'

Pensive they paced along the faded leaves,
While slowly he whose hand held hers replied:
'Passion has often worn our wandering hearts.'

The woods found them, and the yellow leaves
Fell like faint meteors in the gloom, and once
A rabbit old and lame limped down the path;
Autumn was over him: and now they stood
On the lone border of the lake once more:
Turning, he saw that she had thrust dead leaves
Gathered in silence, dewy as her eyes,
In bosom and hair.

'Ah, do not mourn,' he said,
'That we are tired, for other loves await us;
Hate on and love through unrepining hours.
Before us lies eternity; our souls
Are love, and a continual farewell.'

The Ragged Wood

O hurry where by water among the trees
The delicate-stepping stag and his lady sigh,
When they have but looked upon their images—
Would none had ever loved but you and I!

Or have you heard that sliding silver-shoed
Pale silver-proud queen-woman of the sky,
When the sun looked out of his golden hood? —
O that none ever loved but you and I!

O hurry to the ragged wood, for there
I will drive all those lovers out and cry—
O my share of the world, O yellow hair!
No one has ever loved but you and I.

He Wishes His Beloved Were Dead

Were you but lying cold and dead,
And lights were paling out of the West,
You would come hither, and bend your head,
And I would lay my head on your breast;
And you would murmur tender words,
Forgiving me, because you were dead:

Nor would you rise and hasten away,
Though you have the will of the wild birds,
But know your hair was bound and wound
About the stars and the moon and the sun:
O would, beloved, that you lay
Under the dock-leaves in the ground,
While lights were paling one by one.

Reconciliation

Some may have blamed you that you took away
The verses that could move them on the day
When, the ears being deafened, the sight of the eyes blind
With lightening, you went from me, and I could find
Nothing to make a song about but kings,
Helmets, and swords, and half-forgotten things
That were like memories of you—but now
We'll out, for the world lives as long ago;
And while we're in our laughing, weeping fit,
Hurl helmets, crowns, and swords into the pit.
But, dear, cling close to me; since you were gone,
My barren thoughts have chilled me to the bone.

When You Are Old

When you are old and gray and full of sleep,
And nodding by the fire, take down this book,
And slowly read, and dream of the soft look
Your eyes had once, and of their shadows deep;

How many loved your moments of glad grace,
And loved your beauty with love false or true;
But one man loved the pilgrim soul in you
And loved the sorrows of your changing face.

And bending down beside the glowing bars
Murmurs, a little sadly, how love fled
And paced upon the mountains overhead
And hid his face amid a crowd of stars.

For Anne Gregory

'Never shall a young man,
Thrown into despair
By those great honey-colored
Ramparts at your ear,
Love you for yourself alone
And not for your yellow hair.'

'But I can get a hair-dye
And set such color there,
Brown, or black, or carrot,
That young men in despair
May love me for myself alone
And not for my yellow hair.'

'I heard an old religious man
But yesternight declare
That he had found a text to prove
That only God, my dear,
Could love you for yourself alone
And not for your yellow hair.'

Selections From: A Man Young And Old

First Love

Though nurtured like the sailing moon
In beauty's murderous brood,
She walked awhile and blushed awhile
And on my pathway stood
Until I thought her body bore
A heart of flesh and blood.

But since I laid a hand thereon
And found a heart of stone
I have attempted many things
And not a thing is done,
For every hand is lunatic
That travels on the moon.

She smiled and that transfigured me
And left me but a lout,
Maundering here, and maundering there,
Emptier of thought
Than the heavenly circuit of its stars
When the moon sails out.

II
The Mermaid

A mermaid found a swimming lad,
Picked him for her own,
Pressed her body to his body,
Laughed, and plunging down
Forgot in cruel happiness
That even lovers drown.

x
Her Anxiety

Earth in beauty dressed
Awaits returning spring.
All true love must die,
Alter at the best
Into some lesser thing.
Prove that I lie.

Such body lovers have,
Such exacting breath,
That they touch or sigh.
Every touch they give,
Love is nearer death.
Prove that I lie.

Moira O'Neill

The Boy From Ballytearim

He was born in Ballytearim, where there's little work to do,
An' the longer he was livin' there the poorer still he grew;
Says he till all belongin' him, "Now happy may ye be!
But I'm off to find me fortune," sure he says, says he.

"All the gold in Ballytearim is what's stickin' to the whin;
All the crows in Ballytearim has a way o' gettin' thin."
So the people did be praisin' him the year he wint away,—
"Troth, I'll hould ye can do it," sure they says, says they.

Och, the boy 'ud still be thinkin' long an' he across the foam,
An' the two ould hearts be thinkin' long that waited for him home:
But a girl that sat her lone an' whiles, her had upon her knee,
Would be sighin' low for sorra, not a word says she.

He won home to Ballytearim, an' the two were livin' yet,
When he heard where she was lyin' now the eyes of him were wet;
"Faith, here's me two fists full o' gold, an' little good to me
When I'll never meet an' kiss her," sure he says, says he.
Then the boy from Ballytearim set his face another road,
An' whatever luck has followed him was never rightly knowed:
But still it's truth I'm tellin' ye— or may I never sin! —
All the gold in Ballytearim is what's stickin' to the whin.

Thomas MacDonagh

John-John

I dreamt last night of you, John-John,
And thought you called to me;
And when I woke this morning, John,
Yourself I hoped to see;
But I was all alone, John-John,
Though still I heard your call;
I put my boots and bonnet on,
And took my Sunday shawl,
And went full sure to find you, John,
　　At Nenagh fair.

The fair was just the same as then,
Five years ago to-day,
When first you left the thimble-men
And came with me away;
For there again were thimble-men
And shooting galleries,
And card-trick men and maggie-men,
Of all sorts and degrees,
But not a sight of you, John-John,
　　Was anywhere.

I turned my face to home again,
And called myself a fool
To think you'd leave the thimble-men
And live again by rule,
To go to Mass and keep the fast
And till the little patch;
My wish to have you home was past
Before I raised the latch
And pushed the door and saw you, John
　　Sitting down there.

How cool you came in here, begad,
As if you owned the place!
But rest yourself there now, my lad,
'Tis good to see your face;
My dream is out, and now by it
I think I know my mind:
At six o'clock this house you'll quit,

And leave no grief behind; —
But until six o'clock, John-John,
    My bit you'll share.

The neighbors' shame of me began
When first I brought you in;
To wed and keep a tinker man
They thought a kind of sin;
But now this three years since you've gone
'Tis pity me they do,
And that I'd rather have, John-John,
Than that they'd pity you,
Pity for me and you, John-John,
    I could not bear.

Oh, you're my husband right enough,
But what's the good of that?
You know you never were the stuff
To be the cottage cat,
To watch the fire and hear me lock
The door and put out Shep—
But there now, it is six o'clock
And time for you to step.
God bless and keep you far, John-John!
    And that's my prayer.

Joseph Campbell

The Old Woman

As a white candle
  In a holy place,
So is the beauty
  Of an aged face.

As the spent radiance
  Of the winter sun,
So is a woman
  With her travail done.

Her brood gone from her,
  And her thoughts as still
As the waters
  Under a ruined mill.

Pádraig Pearse

Ideal

Naked I saw thee,
O beauty of beauty!
And I blinded my eyes
For fear I should flinch.

I heard thy music,
O sweetness of sweetness!
And I shut my ears
For fear I should fail.

I kissed thy lips
O sweetness of sweetness!
And I hardened my heart
For fear of my ruin.

I blinded my eyes
And my ears I shut,
I hardened my heart
And my love I quenched.

I turned my back
On the dream I had shaped,
And to this road before me
My face I turned.

I set my face
To the road here before me,
To the work that I see,
To the death that I shall meet.

(Translated from the Gaelic by Thomas MacDonagh)

Padraic Colum

River-Mates

I'll be an otter, and I'll let you swim
A mate beside me; we will venture down
A deep, dark river, when the sky above
Is shut of the sun; spoilers are we,
Thick-coated; no dog's tooth can bite at our veins,
With eyes and ears of poachers; deep-earthed ones
Turned hunters; let him slip past
The little vole; my teeth are on an edge
For the King-fish of the River!

    I hold him up
The glittering salmon that smells of the sea;
I hold him high and whistle!
    Now we go
Back to our earths; we will tear and eat
Sea-smelling salmon; you will tell the cubs
I am the Booty-bringer, I am the Lord
Of the River; the deep, dark, full and flowing River!

James Joyce

Tutto È Sciolto

A birdless heaven, seadusk, one lone star
Piercing the west,
As thou, fond heart, love's time, so faint, so far,
Rememberest.

The clear young eyes' soft look, the candid brow,
The fragrant hair,
Falling as through the silence falleth now
Dusk of the air.

Why then, remembering those shy
Sweet lures, repine
When the dear love she yielded with a sigh
Was all but thine?

She Weeps Over Rahoon

Rain on Rahoon falls softly, softly falling,
Where my dark lover lies.
Sad is his voice that calls me, sadly calling,
At grey moonrise.

Love, hear thou
How soft, how sad his voice is ever calling,
Ever unanswered and the dark rain falling,
Then as now.

Dark too our hearts, O love, shall lie and cold
As his sad heart has lain
Under the moongrey nettles, the black mould
And muttering rain.

On The Beach at Fontana

Wind whines and whines the shingle,
The crazy pierstakes groan;
A senile sea numbers each single
Slimesilvered stone.

From whining wind and colder
Grey sea I wrap him warm
And touch his trembling fineboned shoulder
And boyish arm.

Around us fear, descending
Darkness of fear above
And in my heart how deep unending
Ache of love!

Alone

The moon's greygolden meshes make
All night a veil,
The shorelamps in the sleeping lake
Labrunum tendrils trail.

The sly reeds whisper to the night
A name—her name—
And all my soul is a delight,
A swoon of shame.

James Stephens

The Daisies

In the scented bud of the morning—O,
    When the windy grass went rippling far,
I saw my dear one walking slow,
    In the field where the daisies are.
We did not laugh and we did not speak
    As we wandered happily to and fro;
I kissed my dear on either cheek,
    In the bud of the morning—O.

A lark sang up from the breezy land,
    A lark sang down from the cloud afar,
And she and I went hand in hand
    In the field where the daisies are.

Deirdre

Do not let any woman read this verse;
It is for men, and after them their sons
And their sons' sons.

The time comes when our hearts sink utterly;
When we remember Deirdre and her tale,
And that her lips are dust.

Once she did tread the earth; men took her hand;
They looked into her eyes and said their say,
And she replied to them.

More than a thousand years it is since she
Was beautiful: she trod the living grass;
She saw the clouds.

A thousand years! The grass is still the same,
The clouds as lovely as they were that time
When Deirdre was alive.

But there has never been a woman born
Who was so beautiful, not one so beautiful
Of all the women born.

Let all men go apart and mourn together;
No man can ever love her; not a man
Can ever be her lover.

No man can bend before her; no man say—
What could one say to her? There are no words
That one could say to her!

Now she is but a story that is told
Beside the fire! No man can ever be
        The friend of that poor queen.

Austin Clarke

Mable Kelly

Lucky the husband
Who puts his hand beneath her head.
They kiss without scandal
Happiest two near feather-bed.
He sees the tumble of brown hair
Unplait, the breasts, pointed and bare
When nightdress shows
From dimple to toe-nail,
All Mable glowing in it, here, there, and everywhere.

Music might listen
To her least whisper,
Learn every note, for all are true.
While she is speaking,
Her voice goes sweetly
To charm the herons in their musing.
Her eyes are modest, blue, their darkness
Small rooms of thought, but when they sparkle
Upon a feast day,
Glasses are meeting,
Each raised to Mable Kelly, our toast and darling.

Gone now are many Irish ladies
Who kissed and fondled, their very pet-names
Forgotten, their tibia degraded.
She takes their sky. Her smile is famed.
Her praise is scored by quill and pencil.
Harp and spinet
Are in her debt
And when she plays or sings, melody is content.

No man who sees her
Will feel uneasy.
He goes his way, head high, however tired.
Lamp loses light
When placed beside her.

She is the pearl and being all of Ireland
Foot, hand, eye, mouth, breast, thigh, and instep, all that we
    desire.
Tresses that pass small curls as if to touch the ground;
    So many prizes
    Are not divided.
Her beauty is her own and she is not proud.

    (Translation from the Irish)

Frank O'Connor

On The Death Of His Wife

I parted from my life last night,
    A woman's body sunk in clay:
The tender bosom that I loved
    Wrapped in a sheet they took away.

The heavy bosom that had lit
    The ancient boughs is tossed and blown;
Hers was the burden of delight
    That long had weighed the old tree down.

And I am left alone tonight
    And desolate is the world I see
For lovely was that woman's weight
    That even last night had lain on me.

Weeping I look upon the place
    Where she used to rest her head—
For yesterday her body's length
    Reposed upon you too, my bed.

Yesterday that smiling face
    Upon one side of you was laid
That could match the hazel bloom,
    In its dark, delicate, sweet shade.

Maelva of the shadowy brows
    Was the mead-cask at my side;
Fairest of all flowers that grow
    Was the beauty that has died.

My body's self deserts me now,
    The half of me that was her own,
Since all I knew of brightness died
    Half of me lingers, half is gone.

The face that was like hawthorn bloom
    Was my right foot and my right side;
And my right hand and my right eye
    Were no more mine than hers who died

Poor is the share of me that's left
    Since half of me died with my wife;

I shudder at the words I speak;
    Dear God, that girl was half my life.

And our first look was her first love;
    No man had fondled ere I came
The little breasts so small and firm
    And the long body like a flame.

For twenty years we shared a home,
    Our converse milder with each year;
Eleven children in its time
    Did that tall stately body bear.

It was the King of hosts and roads
    Who snatched her from me in her prime:
Little she wished to leave alone
    The man she loved before her time.

Now King of churches and of bells,
    Though never raised to pledge a lie
That woman's hand—can it be true? —
    No more beneath my head will lie.

(Translation from the Irish)

Denis Devlin

Wishes For Her

Against Minoan sunlight
Slight-boned head,
Buildings with the thin climb of larks
Trilling off whetstone brilliants,
Slight head, nor petal nor marble
Night-shell
Two, one and separate.

Love in loving, all
A fledging, hard-billed April,
Soil's gaudy chemistry in fission and fuse.
And she
Lit out of fire and glass
Lightning
The blue flowers of vacant thunder.

In the riverlands
Strained with old battlefields, old armor
In which their child, rust, sighs,
Strangers lost in the courtyard,
I lie awake.
The ice recedes, on black silk
Rocks the seals sway their heads.

No prophet deaths
In the webbed tensions of memory,
No harm
Night lean with hunters.
I wish you well, wish
Tall angels whose rib-freezing
Beauty attends you.

Valentin Iremonger

Hector

Talking to her, he knew it was the end,
The last time he'd speed her to sleep with kisses:
Achilles had it in for him and was fighting mad.
The roads of his longing she again wandered,
A girl desirable as midsummer's day.

He was a marked man and he knew it,
Being no match for Achilles whom the Gods were
    backing.
Sadly he spoke to her for hours, his heart
Snapping like sticks, she on his shoulder crying.
Yet, sorry only that the meaning eluded him.

He slept well at night, having caressed
Andromache like a flower, though in a dream he
    saw
A body lying on the sands, huddled and bleeding,
Near the feet a sword in bits and by the head
An upturned, dented helmet.

John Montague

All Legendary Obstacles

All legendary obstacles lay between
Us, the long imaginary plain,
The monstrous ruck of mountains
And, swinging across the night,
Flooding the Sacramento, San Joaquin,
The hissing drift of winter rain.

All day I wait, shifting
Nervously from station to bar
As I saw another train sail
By, the 'San Francisco Chief' or
'Golden Gate', water dripping
From great flanged wheels.

At midnight you came, pale
Above the negro porter's lamp.
I was too blind with rain
And doubt to speak, but
Reached from the platform
Until our chilled hands met.

You had been traveling for days
With an old lady, who marked
A neat circle on the glass
With her glove, to watch us
Move into the wet darkness
Kissing, still unable to speak.

Pastorals

I

'Lyricize this, my fretful love,
Love is a claw within a velvet glove,
Love is a movement of a withered hand,
Love is a dawn illusion
Blandly planned:
How can brief blood understand?'

II

'Love is the movement of the race
Blood-blindfolded to a chosen face:
Movement of unlawful limbs
In a marriage of two whims:
Consummation of disgrace
Beneath the burning-glass of grace'

III

And yet, my love, we two have come
Into love as to a lighted room
Where all is gaiety and humbling grace.
Hearts long bruised with indolence,
With harsh fatigue of unrelated fact, can trace
Redeeming patterns of experience.

Christy Brown

Lines Of Leaving

I am losing you again
all again
as if you were ever mine to lose.
The pain is as deep
beyond formal possession
beyond the fierce frivolity of tears.

Absurdly you came into my world
my time-wrecked world
a quiet laugh below the thunder.
Absurdly you leave it now
as always I foreknew you would.
I lived on an alien joy.

Your gentleness disarmed me
wine in my desert
peace across impassable seas
path of light in my jungle.

Now uncatchable as the wind you go
beyond the wind
and there is nothing in my world
save the straw of salvation in the amber dream.
The absurdity of that vast improbable joy.
The absurdity of you gone.

What Her Absence Means

It means
    no madcap delight will intrude
into the calm flow of my working hours
    no ecstatic errors perplex
my literary pretensions.

It means
    there will be time enough for thought
undistracted by brown peril of eye
    and measured litany of routine deeds
undone by the ghost of a scent.

It means
    my neglect of the Sonnets will cease
and Homer come into battle once more.
    I might even find turgid old Tennyson
less of a dead loss now.

It means
    there will be whole days to spare
for things important to a man—
    like learning to live without a woman
without altogether losing one's mind.

It means
    there is no one now to read my latest poem
with veiled unhurried eyes
    putting my nerves on the feline rack
in silence sheer she-devil hell for me.

It means
    there is no silly woman to tell me
"Take it easy—life's long anyway—
don't drink too much—get plenty of sleep—"
    and other tremendous clichés.

It means
    I am less interrupted now with love.

Tom Mac Intyre

On Sweet Killen Hill

Flower of the flock,
Any time, any land,
Plenty your ringlets,
Plenty your hand,
Sunlight your window,
Laughter your sill,
And I must be with you
On sweet Killen Hill.

Let sleep renegue me,
Skin lap my bones,
Love and Tomorrow
Can handle the reins.

You my companion
I'd never breathe ill,
And I guarantee bounty
On sweet Killen Hill.

You'll hear the pack yell
As puss devil-dances,
Hear cuckoo and thrush
Pluck song from the branches,
See fish in the pool
Doing their thing,
And the bay as God made it
From sweet Killen Hill.

Pulse of my life,
We come back to—'Mise.'
Why slave for McArdle
That bumbaliff's issue?
I've a harp in a thousand,
Love songs at will,
And the air is Cadenza
On sweet Killen Hill.

Gentle one, lovely one,
Come to me,
Now sleep the clergy,
Now sleep their care,
Sunrise will find us
But sunrise won't tell
That love lacks surveillance
On sweet Killen Hill.

(Translation from the Irish)

James Simmons

The End Of The Affair

We could count the times we went for a walk
or the times we danced together in the past
months—if not the times of making love and talk.
Our first separation will be our last.

I suppose we never discussed what we have known:
that I am to go home, that you will stay.
All the mutual tenderness that has grown,
sweet as it is, is not to get in the way

of the work before us, mine and yours.
What has been given us is being taken away,
and we aren't looking for loopholes and cures,
freely absenting ourselves from this felicity

to tell our story under plain covers
in bed, or by example, till everyone understands
that joy will not be bound. Artists and lovers
start and complete their work with empty hands.

To leave my wife and children for love's sake
and marry you would be a failure of nerve.
I remember love and all that goes to make
the marriage, the affairs, that I deserve.

A Long Way After Ronsard
(FOR EILEEN)

When the time has made you wrinkled, sore and slow,
and let my caged abilities fly free,
will you feel proud when many people know
I longed for you and you rejected me?

Deaf to my wit, my anger and my prayers,
you didn't even want to lead me on.
Those nights frustration hounded me upstairs
and kept the pencil in my hand till dawn.

Reading those poems will you see how vile
you were to me, and what a paltry choice
he was—that smoother man? Or will you smile,
'Poor Jim is famous?'...I can hear your voice.

Desmond O'Grady

In the Greenwood

I

My darling, my love,
    Together let's rove
Through the forest so flagrantly scenting.
    By trout streams we'll rest,
    Watch the thrush build her nest,
While the buck and the roe buck are calling.
    Each ring singing bird
    In the wild wind wood heard
And the cuckoo high up in the plane trees
    And never will come
    Death into our home
In the shade of the sweet smelling green-trees.

II

    O beautiful head
    All kiss curled red,
Green and grand your eyes are;
    My heart is high-strung,
    Like a thread too well spun.
From loving too long from afar.

(Translation from the Irish)

Brendan Kennelly

Bread

Someone else cut off my head
In a golden field.
Now I am re-created

By her fingers. This
Moulding is more delicate
Than a first kiss,

More deliberate than her own
Rising up
And lying down.

I am fine
As anything in
This legendary garden

Even at my weakest, I am
Finer than anything
In this legendary garden

Yet I am nothing till
She runs her fingers through me.
And shapes me with her skill.

The form that I shall bear
Grows round and white.
It seems I comfort her

Even as she slits my face
And stabs my chest.
Her feeling for perfection is

Absolute.
So I am glad to go through fire
And come out

Shaped like her dream.
In my way
I am all that can happen to men.
I came to life at her fingerends
I will go back into her again.

Seamus Heaney

A New Song

I met a girl from Derrygarve
And the name, a lost potent musk,
Recalled the river's long swerve,
A kingfisher's blue bolt at dusk

And stepping stones like black molars
Sunk in the ford, the shifty glaze
Of the whirlpool, the Moyola
Pleasuring beneath alder trees.

And Derrygarve, I thought, was just,
Vanished music, twilit water,
A smooth liberation of the past
Poured by this chance vestal daughter.

But now our river tongues must rise
From licking deep in native haunts
To flood, with vowelling embrace,
Demesnes staked out in consonants.

And Castledawson we'll enlist
And Upperlands, each planted bawn—
Like bleaching-greens resumed by grass—
A vocable, as rath and bullaun.

Caitlín Maude

Entanglement

Walk, my love,
by the strand tonight—
walk, and away
with tears—
arise and walk tonight

henceforth never bend your knee
at that mountain grave
those flowers have withered
and my bones decayed...

(I speak to you tonight
from the bottom of the sea—
I speak to you each night
from the bottom of the sea...)

once I walked on the strand—
I walked to the tide's edge—
wave played with wave—
the white foam licked my feet—
I slowly raised my eye
and there far out on the deep
in the tangle of foam and wave
I saw the loneliness in your eye
the sorrow in your face

I walked out on the deep
from knee to waist
and from waist to shoulder
until I was swallowed
in sorrow and loneliness

(Translated by Gabriel Fitzmaurice)

Vietnam Love Song

They said that we were shameless
celebrating our love
with devastation all around us

the hawk hovering in the air
awaiting the stench of death
they said that these were our own
that this was the funeral of our own people
that we should at least be solemn
even if we were not mourning

but we
we are like the weather
          especially the sun
we don't pay much attention
to these happenings any longer

everything decays in the heat of the sun
after death

and it wasn't we who killed them
but you

we could have stayed on the field of slaughter
but the sad faces of the soldiers
made us laugh
and we chose a soft place by the river

(Translated by Gabriel Fitzmaurice)

Entreaty

Young man,
do not come near me,
do not speak...
the words of love
are sweet—
but sweeter still
is the word
that was never uttered—
no choice
is without stain—
the choice of words

is much the same
and this would be
to choose between evils
in our present
situation...

   Do not break
   the clear glass
   between us
      (no glass is broken
      without blood and pain)
for beyond is Heaven
or beyond is Hell
and what good is Heaven
if it is not
for ever? —
the loss of
Heaven
is the worst Hell...

I again implore you,
do not speak,
young man,
my 'Diarmaid,'
and we will be at peace—
untouchable understanding
between us
we will have no cause
to touch it
ever
as it ever
allures us—
but I implore you...
do not speak...

(Translated by Gabriel Fitzmaurice)

John F. Deane

Sacrament

You, pictured for ever, before me;
I stand in black and wear a white
carnation; you, holding an array
of golden roses, maidenhair, smile up
at me and you are beautiful; your body
washed for me and gently scented;
you, set apart in white, a mystery,
all sacred:
        we are holding hands for ever,
dedicated; such are the signs of a deep
abiding grace.

          Another image
graven on my mind; you lie, again
in white; on your breast a silken
picture of the Virgin; they have washed
your body, closed your eyes, you hold
no flowers; vein-blue traces
of suffering on your skin, your fingers
locked together, away from me.

But it is I who have loved you, known
the deepest secrets of your grace; I take
the golden ring from your finger; I kiss
the bride,

      and they close the heavy doors
against me, of that silent, vast cathedral.

Augustus Young

Woman, Don't Be Troublesome

Woman, don't be troublesome,
though your husband I may be;
our two minds were once at one,
why withdraw your hand from me.

Put your mouth of strawberry
on my mouth, cream is your cheek;
wind round white arms about me,
and do not go back to sleep.

Stay with me my flighty maid,
and be done with betrayal;
tonight this bed is wellmade,
let us toss it without fail.

Shut your eyes to other men,
no more women will I see:
the milkwhite tooth of passion
is between us—or should be.

(Translation from the Irish)

Paul Durcan

She Mends An Ancient Wireless

You never claimed to be someone special;
Sometimes you said you had no special talent;
Yet I have seen you rear two dancing daughters
With care and patience and love unstinted;
Reading or telling stories, knitting gansies
And all the while holding down a job
In the teeming city, morning until dusk.
And in the house whenever anything went wrong
You were the one who fixed it without fuss;
The electricity switch which was neither on nor off,
The TV aerial forever falling out;
And now as I watch you mend an ancient wireless
From my tiny perch I cry once more your praises
And call out your name across the great divide—Nessa.

Gabriel Rosenstock

The Search
(For My Wife, Eithne)

Where are the poems I promised
I would write for you?
They are not in ink—

You will find them in the foam of rivers
In the seas
In the vapor above clifftops
In the swirling breeze
In eagles' eyes
In the clouds
In the skies
Even in the stars
On their eternal journey
From void to void.
They are not in print—

The flowers' sweetness snatched them
While you hunkered in the garden.
Nettles burned them
Dock soothed them
Ladybirds landed on them
And walked like critics
Seeking rhyme and metre.
They even failed to find a title. For who
Could put a name on you!
With every breath.
I name you.
Where are all the verbs?
You have gathered them to yourself.
The adjectives?
Nestling in your breast.
Punctuation?
It adorns you.
Nouns, vowels, consonants,
The Irish language, its sound and sense,
I dedicate to you, Eithne.

II

From age to age I seek your shape
Like a winglet
Like a leaf.
When we are children,
Heroes,
And elders,
On death's cold stone
And in the womb,
Every moment
Shapes my poem—
It ever welcomes you.
Can you hear the gale?
The world turns
And all is turning,
The hills and the peaks above them.
We closed our eyes, and opened them,
Then closed them again in wonder.

III

Do not greet me
Do not look at me
Do not seek me
I escape
I seek you
We do not exist
In any time
In any place
We are not in the realms of words
Or love
(Although our love is strong).
Take my hand,
Love; hear the heart's tympany
That beat long ago for you and me,
That we still don't understand.

(Translated by Gabriel Fitzmaurice)

Medbh McGuckian

On Not Being Your Lover

Your eyes were ever brown, the colour
Of time's submissiveness. Love nerves
Or a heart, beat in their world of
Privilege, I had not yet kissed you
On the mouth.

But I would not say, in my un-freedom
I had weakly drifted there, like the
Bone-deep blue that visits and decants
The eyes of our children:

How warm and well-spaced their dreams
You can tell from the sleep-late mornings
Taken out of my face! Each lighted
Window shows me cardigained, more desolate
Than the garden, and more hallowed
Than the hinge of the brass-studded
Door that we close, and no one opens,
That we open and no one closes.

In a far-flung, too young part,
I remembered all your slender but
Persistent volume said, friendly, complex
As the needs of your new and childfree girl.

The Sofa

Do not be angry if I tell you
Your letter stayed unopened on my table
For several days. If you were friend enough
To believe me, I was about to start writing
At any moment; my mind was savagely made up,
Like a serious sofa moved
Under a north window. My heart, alas,

Is not the calmest of places.
Still it is not my heart that needs replacing:
And my books seem real enough to me,
My disasters, my surrenders, all my loss...
Since I was child enough to forget
That you loathe poetry, you ask for some—
About nature, greenery, insects, and of course,

The sun—surely that would be to open
An already open window? Celebrating
The impudence of flowers? If I could
Interest you instead in his large, gentle stares,
How his soft shirt is the inside of pleasure
To me, why I must wear white for him,
Imagine he no longer trembles

When I approach, no longer buys me
Flowers for my name day. . . But I spread
On like a house, I begin to scatter
To a tiny to-and-fro at odds
With the wear on my threshold. Somewhere
A curtain rising wonders where I am,
My books sleep, pretending to forget me.

Fred Johnston

For Emma

Your name has a biblical ring
in this city of biblethumpers and Old
Testament cruelties
two syllables singing like a bell

I'd spray your name and mine on a
gable-end, scratch our initials in
a 'phone-box,' as good as a fire on the
Cave Hill for the whole city to see

child of the dustbin territories, their
tinlid tattoo entered your ears at birth
echoes in the anteroom of the heart
even now, like the memory of a first kiss

you've worn it well, Emma,
the handed-down tattery shawl of tribal
suffering
you will never turn it into a flag

or hide beneath it. No it's in your
voice, the frank shape of your mouth
they have painted no slogans on any wall
in our town to describe how you feel

at all times your beauty is more precious
than their violence, the men who have made
your dreams unsafe
squalid ghosts, fleshy myths

We Are Rivers, Frozen

There is a notion that time has passed
a considerable length of time
and that we have become two persons
each quite changed and grown wiser

there is a strict myth to be observed
how we've grown to understandings
mutual affections but no real concern
how we've learned to take it on the chin

and also there is what the others say
was best, and it is easy to obey
take orders when the heart is numb:
there is the ritual of passing by

I have taken all I can from the high-
priests of consolation and sacrifice:
be firm, they said, leaving me alone
and losing hold

I have waited as long as I dare for
some evidence that what we shared is
remembered and may be revived: this
is almost a religion, the need of faith

blinds all other concerns. This is
our winter and we are rivers, frozen—
too much wisdom has consumed the flame
when I was innocent there was magic in your name.

Paul Muldoon

Something Of A Departure

Would you be an angel
And let me rest,
This one last time,
Near that plum-colored beauty spot
Just below your right buttock?

Elizabeth, Elizabeth,
Had words not escaped us both
I would have liked to hear you sing
'Farewell to Tarwathie'
Or 'Ramble Away.'

Your thigh, your breast,
Your wrist, the ankle
That might yet sprout a wing—
You're altogether as slim
As the chance of our meeting again.

So put your best foot forward
And steady, steady on.
Show me the plum-colored beauty spot
Just below your right buttock,
And take it like a man.

Gabriel Fitzmaurice

Garden

(For Brenda)

We were a garden dug by eager hands.
Weeds were swept by shovels underground.
Brown earth, blackened and split by Winter,
Was picked to a skeleton by starving birds.

Spring surprised us with a yelp of daisies
Defiant as a terrier guarding his home ground.
We planted seed in the cleft of drills
Slimy with earthworms.

Today I picked the first fruit of our garden.
Bloody with earth I offered it to you
     You washed it and anointed it,
     We ate it like viaticum.

     In the eating of pith and seed
     I loved you.

In The Midst Of Possibility

Now I love you
Free of me:
In this loving I can see
The YOU of you
Apart from me—
The YOU of you that's ever free.

This is the YOU I love.
This is the YOU I'll never have:
This is the YOU beyond possession—

The YOU that's ever true
While ever changing,
Ever new.

Now,
Naked
Free,
The YOU of you
Meets the ME of me
And to see is to love;
To love, to see:

In the midst of possibility
We agree.

Nuala Ní Dhomhnaill

Labasheedy (The Silken Bed)

I'd make a bed for you
in Labasheedy
in the tall grass
under the wrestling trees
where your skin
would be silk upon silk
in the darkness
when the moths are coming down.

Skin which glistens
shining over your limbs
like milk being poured
from jugs at dinnertime;
your hair is a herd of goats
moving over rolling hills,
hills that have high cliffs
and two ravines.

And your damp lips
would be as sweet as sugar
at evening and we walking
by the riverside
with honeyed breezes
blowing over the Shannon
and the fuchsias bowing down to you
one by one.

The fuchsias bending low
their solemn heads
in obeisance to the beauty
in front of them
I would pick a pair of flowers
as pendant earrings
to adorn you
like a bride in shining clothes.

O, I'd make a bed for you
in Labasheedy,
in the twilight hour
with evening falling slow
and what a pleasure it would be
to have our limbs entwine
wrestling
while the moths are coming down.

(Translated by the author)

Jo Slade

When Our Heads Bend

When our heads bend,
We kiss.
We excite the deer
In her quiet wood,
We draw the hare
From his burrow.

Sara Berkeley

The Parting

I

You lower my emotions, sealed in their casket,
To the sea bed, knowing I have nothing to say
Paring down to presence and absence
The sad abstractions of our last day
My throat grows heavy between your hands
My heart gets tossed away.

2

A shadow is working hard against the night
Working furiously on a morning wall
The shadow cast by fifteen beams of light
I am a child's bright stone
Longing to be the weapon of your fight
I am the fifteen beams coming straight down.

3

In brief moments when a nerve winks out
It seems as though you will always be there
The heart kicks — and then you are removed
You are climbing down the angry white stairs
You are the shadow resting on my skin
And we, a double splash of oars into the still air.

Glenda Cimino

The Unwed Wife
(For Brian)

Four a.m. The coldest hour. Our child sleeps beside me,
her soft petal breath warming the sheets
where you have been. She entitles me to nothing;
her whole being radiates love.

After six months absence, the pillow again
smells sweetly of you. But for five nights
I have gone to sleep and woken without you,
When will I stop counting the lonely nights?

I sleep in my clothes and dream of nakedness
with you. My dream of you is your best part.
The day I stop dreaming you, you will surely disappear.
You don't know how my dreams keep you going.

My powerful woman's magic draws you near
when the moon is full, as moon draws sea,
as its power causes solid land to ebb and flow,
imperceptibly ... In the space between wish and lie

Is my poem's truth. Our daughter's hand holds the blanket,
the tilt of her chin so like yours.
Beside the bed, the book you were reading and a peach,
perfect in light and shadow as a Rembrandt.

Tonight I have locked the doors; I am too far away
to hear your knock, real or imagined.
Sirius in his own lonely exile guards our door.
I think of reading the book. Eating the peach.

Outside the trees stretch in the wind.
Without you we always sleep in the light.
Darkness may not penetrate our white sanctuary.
When you come you bring darkness, want the light off,

You wear your pain like a skin you cannot remove,
you are always on the prongs of a dilemma.
You never love me enough to stay;
I don't know why you come.

But tonight, where your head rested,
your smell sweetly scents the pillow.
Soon, in the gray morning, I must arise
and wash it away.

Mary O'Malley

Aftermath
For Mike

Last night I looked at you,
A stark man in this gray country
Of short days and long nightfalls.
I watched and marveled
That you should still be here,
For I had not seen you much
In the storms of these past years.

Time and God and bureaucrats
Have pared us both down
To some of our essentials,
With deft little secateurs
Or blunt edgeless implements,
Such as are sought in murder hunts.

Each inflicted its own pain
As it peeled back, gouged
Or merely hacked away
To reach and reveal a deeper layer,
Here a terra cotta shard
Of smashed solicitude,
There a flint of fear,

Perhaps even a purple thread,
Last remnant of some glorious bolt
Of desire. Such delvings and exhumations
Seldom yield the unbroken,
Though sometimes beautiful tokens
Are taken out of their darkness
To be exposed to the light in museums.

They have left me with furrows
And ridges that no coyness
Can rechristen laughter lines.
Yet you are still here;

And I watching
Wondered if I would ever know
This defined and distant man
That I have lived beside
As I knew the boy
The instant the air shifted between us,
Moments after we met.

Author Biographies

Nahum Tate (1652-1715) was born and educated in Dublin. He began his writing career as a playwright and became Poet Laureate in 1692. He wrote only one original poem that lasted past his death: *Panacea: a Poem Upon Tea* (1700).

George Farquhar (1678-1707) was born in Derry and educated at Trinity College, Dublin. He enjoyed moderate success in Ireland as an actor, before he left for London where he began writing plays. These scripts were complete failures and Farquhar remained penniless for most of his life. His first success occurred in 1707 with the advent of his play entitled, *Les Beaux Stratagem*.

Oliver Goldsmith (1728-1774), journalist, dramatist, and poet, was born in Pallasmore, County Longford. After attempting Edinburgh University for two years, he left school to travel Europe on foot. He arrived in London in 1756 and began publishing anonymously such satirical observations as *The Citizen of the World* (1762). The first work to bear his name was *The Travelers: A Prospect of Society* (1765). He continued writing and gaining fame, although his thrifty and generous nature caused him to remain penniless even at the height of his popularity. His other works include *The Good Natured Man: A Comedy* (1768) and *She Stoops to Conquer* (1773).

Richard Brinsley Sheridan (1751-1816) was born in Dublin and began his career as a playwright at the suggestion of the manager of the Convent Garden Theater. In 1780, he was elected to Parliament and maintained employment with the Government until 1812. Falling into grave debt, he became a chronic alcoholic and in 1816 took his own life.

Thomas Moore (1779-1852) was born and educated in Dublin as both a poet and a musician. His voice and musical ability made him a preferred guest of the British aristocracy. After a brief time as the Admiralty Registrar in Bermuda, he traveled to London and America. He continued to establish himself as a writer along the way through many verse collections and tales. These works confirmed his growing reputation as an Irish national bard. His other works include *The Fudge Family in Paris* (1818), *Memoirs of Captain Rock* (1824), *Irish Melodies* (1807-1834), and *Epistles, Odes and Other Poems* (1806).

Charles Wolfe (1792-1823) was born in County Clare and educated at the

Hyde Abbey School, Winchester and Dublin. He is commemorated for his religious services at St. Patrick's Cathedral in Dublin. His most famous poem is *The Burial of Sir Thomas Moore.*

William Maginn (1793-1842) was born in Cork and received his education in Dublin. He was a frequent contributor to many London periodicals and became famous for his humorous stories and parodies. He also co-founded the literary review, *Frazer's Magazine.*

Samuel Lover (1797-1868) was born and educated in Dublin. In 1833, he and a few colleagues founded the highly successful literary periodical *Dublin University Magazine.* After a number of years of writing for the magazine, he left for London where he found great success in the entertainment business. His farcical novel, *Handy Andy,* is his best known work.

Gerald Griffen (1803-1840) was born in Limerick and received his education locally. After his parents emigrated to the United States in 1820, he continued to live in Ireland with his older brother. In 1823, after beginning his writing career in Ireland, he left for London to earn a living. Reflecting his own modest tast, his writings often revolved around 19th century Irish provincial life. In 1838, he destroyed his manuscripts and joined the teaching order of the Christian Brothers in Dublin, dying of typhus at the monastery in Cork. His other works include *The Rivals* (1830), *Tracey's Ambition* (1830), and *Tales of My Neighborhood* (1835).

James Clarence Mangan (1803-1849) was born in Dublin and known throughout his life as an eccentric. In 1834, he, like fellow writers Samuel Ferguson, John Francis Waller and much later W.B. Yeats, began contributing to the *Dublin University Magazine.* He developed a nationalistic passion for Irish material. In 1842, he began contributing as a salaried writer to the *Nation* (founder/editor Sir Charles Gavan Duffy). He spent the last years of his life as an alcoholic and died in a cholera epidemic. Other works include: *The Dubliner: The Lives, Times, and Writings of James Clarance Mangan* (1888); his best known poem is entitled *Dark Rosaleen.*

Helen Lady Selina Dufferin (1807-1867) was the granddaughter of Richard Brinsley Sheridan. She wrote both poetry and satirical verse.

John Francis Waller (1810-1894) (a.k.a. Jonathan Freke Slingsby) was born in Limerick, Ireland. He worked as both a journalist and an editor on the *Dublin University Magazine* (founded by Samuel Lover). His most well-known works include: *The Slingsby Papers* (1852) and *Occasional Odes* (1864).

Sir Samuel Ferguson (1810-1886) was born in Belfast, and educated at the Academical Institution, Belfast, and Trinity College, Dublin. Studying law in school, he was called to the Irish Bar (1838) and later appointed to the Queen's Counsel (1859). He contributed to magazines such as *Dublin University* and *Blackwood's Edinburgh*, using his literary talents to promote peace and understanding between the Catholic and Protestant factions of Ireland. He gained fame as a translator of both Gaelic legends and sagas, however, his works disputed many nationalistic notions popular at the time. His most famous works include *Lays of the Western Gale and Other Poems* (1865) and *Congal: A Poem in Five Books* (1872).

Aubrey de Vere (1814-1902) was born in Curragh Chase, County Limerick. He received his degree at Trinity College, Dublin. Although he took orders in the Anglican Church (later converting to Roman Catholicism), he studied literature and philosophy instead of theology. He then traveled to London where he met and spent time with both Tennyson and Wordsworth. His first published work was *English Misrule and Irish Misdeeds* (1848). *The Foray of Queen Maeve* (1882) is regarded as the most impressive and interesting of his poetical works.

Sir Charles Gavan Duffy (1816-1903) was born in Monaghan, Ireland. He became a journalist in Dublin and Belfast. In 1842, he founded *The Nation*, the famous nationalist paper which published many of the writings of members of the Young Irish Movement and helped the Irish Literary Revival. After the collapse of the group, he was tried for sedition and later died in Nice, France.

Denis Florence MacCarthy (1817-1882) was born, lived, and died in Dublin. He became a noted translator, professor and poet of Irish ballads. He was saluted by the Irish as Ireland's own Poet Laureate, the only true successor of Thomas Moore as the Irish National Bard. His other works include *Ballads, Poems, and Lyrics* (1880), and *Shelley's Early Life* (1872).

William Allingham (1824-1889) was born in Ballyshannon, County Donegal, and educated at a boarding school in County Cavan. Eventually, he left Ireland and his father's banking business to find his way in the literary circles of London. In 1870, he became editor of the famous London literary magazine, *Frazer's*.

Charles Kickham (1828-1882) was born in Mullinahoure, County Tipperary. As a young man, he began taking an active part in the Young Ireland Movement and in 1860 became a Fenian. As editor of the newspaper, *The*

Irish People, he found a forum for his strong nationalistic beliefs and writings about Irish life. His novel, *Knockagon* (1879), is recognized as his best work. Other works include *Poems, Sketches and Narratives* (1870), and *For the Old Land* (1886).

Charles Graham Halpine (1829-1868) (a.k.a. Miles O'Reilly) was born in Oldcastle, County Meath. He graduated from Trinity College and turned to journalism as his career. In 1851, he immigrated to America and distinguished himself in the American Civil War. He died at age 39 from an accidental overdose of chloroform. His well-known poems include *The Patriot Brothers, Mount Cashels Brigade,* and *Lyrics By the Letter H* (1854).

John Boyle O'Reilly (1844-1890) was born in Dowth Castle, County Meath. He became a soldier in the British Army and continued his military duties as transporter in the Fenian movement. He later escaped to the United States, where he spent the rest of his life. His works include *In Bohemia* (1886) and *The Statues in the Block* (1884).

Isabella Valancy Crawford (1850-1887) was born in Dublin but emigrated to the United States with her parents as a young girl. After a difficult childhood, she and her mother settled in Toronto where Crawford contributed stories to many American and Canadian magazines. Her only book to be published during her lifetime was *Old Spookses' Pass, Malcolm's Katie* and *Other Poems* (1884). However, despite favorable reviews in both countries, it sold poorly.

George Moore (1852-1933) was born in Ballyglass, County Mayo. He received his education at Oscott College, Birmingham and was best known as a novelist and critic. After graduating, he left his home to live in Paris. Failing as a painter, he turned his talents to the world of literature. His first published works were 2 volumes of verse called *Flowers of Passion* (1878) and *Pagen Poems* (1881). He later returned to Dublin and helped Yeats manage the Irish Literary Theater renamed the Abbey Theater. He then returned to London in 1911 and began publishing exposés of the Irish Literary Revival and Irish Catholicism.

William Drummond (1854-1907) is still counted among the lists of Irish poets, despite his emigration to Canada as a young boy. Born in Currawn, County Leitrim, he received his education at McGill and Bishop's University where he went on to become a doctor. After completing his degree in 1884, he worked in the mining camps in Montreal, incorporating both the French-Canadian language and culture that he encountered into his poetry (*The Habitant;* 1897). He died of a stroke in 1907.

Katherine Tynan (1861-1931) was born in County Dublin. She began writing poetry as a young woman, publishing her first work in 1885. She became a member of the Irish Literary Revival, joining the ranks of fellow poets Joseph Campbell and Sir Charles Gavan Duffy, upon the publishing of her book entitled Innocencies (1905). The themes of her later poems rely heavily upon her thoughts and experiences during her travels throughout Europe. Her other works include *Life in the Occupied Area* (1925), *Twenty-Five Years* (1913), *The Wandering Years* (1923), and *Poems* (1963).

William Butler Yeats (1865-1939) is one of Ireland's best known and loved poets, often referred to as the "only poet born with manners." He was born in Sandymount, Dublin. Although his family moved to London in 1867, he returned to Ireland in 1880 to attend school.As a young idealistic revolutionary, he met and developed a life-long love and admiration for the actress and Irish nationalist, Maud Gonne. Many of his poems revolve around his respect and unrequited love for her, often comparing her to the Greek Helen. He was one of the initiators of the Irish renaissance or the Irish Literary Revival and founded the Irish National Theater (later renamed the Abbey Theater) in 1897. He was awarded the Nobel Prize for literature in 1923. He refuted the ideas of complex and flowery language in poetry in exchange for the use of common everyday words. His best works are included in the following collections: *Yeat's Poems* (1989), *Poems and Ballads of Young Ireland* (1889), The Wind Among the Reeds (1899), *In the Seven Woods* (1903), and *The Green Helmet and Other Poems* (1910).

Moira O'Neill was born in Cushindall, County Antrim. She spent most of her adult life in County Wexford, Ireland. Her first published work, *Songs from the Glens of Antrim*, appeared in 1900. It was reissued in the United States in 1922 as *More Songs of The Glens of Antrimz.*

Thomas MacDonagh (1878-1916) was born near Tipperary and received his education at the National University. He went on to become a contributor to the newly founded political forum, *Irish Review*. After taking an active part in the 1916 Easter Rising, his revolutionary ways and ideas led to his, and fellow poet Pádraig Pearse's, execution. His poetry appears, posthumously, in *Poetical Works* (1917).

Joseph Campbell (1879-1944) was born in Belfast. At the turn of the century, he followed many of his fellow artisans, such as Katherine Tynan and W.B. Yeats, to Dublin to participate in the Irish Literary Revival. Throughout his life he spent time both in London and the United States. He founded the School of Irish Studies in New York and the *Irish Review*. Returning to

Wicklow, Ireland in 1939, he finished his life a lonely man. His other works include *Irishry* (1913) and *Earth of Cualann* (1917).

Pádraig Pearse (1880-1916) was born and educated in Dublin, receiving his degree from University College of Galway. He was editor of the Gaelic League's weekly journal (1903-1909) and crusaded throughout Ireland for the return of the Gaelic language to modern literature. In 1908, he established St. Edna's school for the teaching of Irish. His revolutionary themes and separatist beliefs, including those in support of force and violence, appear throughout his poetry. He, along with Thomas MacDonagh, was executed for his actions in the 1916 Easter Rising.

Padraic Colum (1881-1972) was born in Longford, Ireland and educated at Glasthule National School, Sandycove. He worked as a railways clerk until age 22, when he was given a five-year scholarship to pursue his writing career. He, along with Yeats, was a founding member of the Abbey Theater. In 1914, he and his wife emigrated to the United States where he continued his work in poetry, adding children's stories and the retellings of both Classical and Irish legends to his repertoire. His best known works include *The Wild Earth and Other Poems* (1907), *Flying Swans* (1957), and *The Poet's Circuits: Collected Poems of Ireland* (1960).

James Joyce (1882-1941), next to William Butler Yeats, is one of Ireland's best-known authors. He was born in Dublin, although he spent the majority of his life (after 1902) traveling and living abroad. Throughout his life he returned to Ireland only once. However, all of his books are set in Ireland. He received his education at Jesuit Belvedere College. His first published work was a collection of short lyrical poems called *Chamber Music* (1907). His writing brought him little money and he existed almost solely on the assistance of his patrons. Better known as an author of prose, his books include Dubliners (1914), *A Portrait of an Artist as A Young Man* (1916), *Ulyssess* (1922) and *Finnegan's Wake* (1939).

James Stephens (1882-1950) was born in Dublin and placed in an orphanage as a young boy. His early works illustrated the plight of the Irish urban poor while his later works attempted to mesh both the rural Irish pleasures with the heroic fairy-tales from his youth. His works include *Insurrections* (1909), *The Crock of Gold* (1912), *Deirdre* (1923) and *In the Land of Youth* (1924).

Austin Clarke (1896-1974) is celebrated as one of Ireland's finest national poets of the twentieth century. He was born in Dublin and educated at the Jesuit Belvedere College and University College, Dublin, where he received his M.A. and worked as an English lecturer from 1918-1922. Clarke was a founding member of the Irish Academy of Letters. His early works, such as *The Violence of Fionn* (1917), attempted to recreate the Celtic atmosphere. He enjoyed fame as a national poet for his concern (and satire) on the contradictions of modern Irish life as well as the adaptation and revival of traditional poetic forms. Other works include *Selected Poems* (1992) and *Twice Round the Black Church* (1962).

Frank O'Connor (1902-1966) (a.k.a. Michael O'Donovan) was born in Cork to a poor family. By the age of 12 he had left school. He was imprisoned for his political activities during the civil war, many of which are reflected in his first volume of stories. He went on to become active in literary circles as both a critic and writer. He directed the Abbey Theater from 1935-1939. He published original short stories and his own translations of Irish poetry. His translations are included in his work: *Kings, Lords and Commons: An Anthology from the Irish* (1959).

Denis Devlin (1908-1959) was born in Greenock, Scotland, but returned with his family to Ireland as a young boy. Receiving his education at Belvedere and University College, Dublin, he proved himself to be a master at languages. Utilizing his language skills, he went on to join the Irish Foreign Service holding many important diplomatic posts. He has translated and written numerous collections of poetry including *Poems* (1930), *Intercessions* (1937), *Translations into English* (1992), and *Collected Poems* (1990).

Valentin Iremonger (b. 1918) was born in Dublin and received his education at Synge Street Christian Brothers School, Colaiste Mhuire and the Abbey Theater School of Acting (1938-1940). Following in the footsteps of fellow poet, Denis Devlin, he served in the Irish Foreign Service, holding posts throughout the years as Irish Ambassador to India, Luxembourg, and many of the Scandinavian countries. He was also the poetry editor of *Envoy* magazine in Dublin and the author of many articles and reviews in both Irish and British journals. As a writer and translator, his works appear in On the *Barricades* (1944), *Reservations, Beatha Mhuire* (1950), *Horan's Field and Other Reservations* (1972).

John Montague (b. 1929), despite his Stateside birth in Brooklyn, New York, spent most of his childhood in County Tyrone and received his education at University College, Dublin. He has been both a journalist and teacher. His first book of poetry was called *Farms of Exile* (1958). Other works include *The Rough Field* (1972), *A Slow Dance* (1975), *The Dead Kingdom* (1984), *Selected Poems* (1982), and *New Selected Poems* (1990).

Christy Brown (1932-1981) was born in Dublin to a large family. Almost completely paralyzed from birth, Brown overcame his handicap to type his autobiography, *My Left Foot* (1954), with his little toe. Although his writing is uneven, and sporadic, few works can compare to the courage, determination, and power of his autobiography. Other works include *Down All the Days* (1970), *Come Softly to My Wake* (1970), and *Collected Poems* (new edition 1990).

Tom Mac Intyre (b. 1933) was born in County Cavan and received his education at University College, Dublin. He has taught at universities in both Ireland and America. He now bases himself in Dublin, and is heavily involved in theater. He enjoys success as a writer of both drama and poetry. His other works include: *The Charollais* (1969), *Dance the Dance* (1970), *I Bailed Out at Ardee* (1987) and *The Great Hunger* (1988).

James Simmons (b. 1933) was born in Derry, Northern Ireland. He received his degree from Leeds University, England. He taught in both Ireland and Nigeria for many years. Upon returning to Ireland, he began a literary magazine called *Honest Ulsterman*. His other works include *Late but in Earnest* (1967), *In the Wilderness* (1969), *The Long Summer Still to Come* (1973), *From the Irish* (1985), and *Poems 1956-1986* (1986).

Desmond O'Grady (b. 1935) was born in County, Limerick and educated at University College Dublin and Harvard University. He has published both original poetry and poetry in translation. He now lives in Kinsale, County Cork. His collections include *The Dark Edge of Europe* (1967), *Off License* (1968), *Separations* (1973), and *The Headgear of the Tribe* (1979).

Brendan Kennelly (b. 1936) was born in Ballylongford, County Kerry and received his education at St. Ida's College, Tarbet, Trinity College, Dublin and Leeds University. He began publishing his work in 1959. His collections of poetry include *Getting Up Early* (1966), *Dream of a Black Fox* (1968), *Bread* (1971), *Love Cry* (1972), and *A Time for Voices: Selected Poems 1960-1990* (1990).

Seamus Heaney (b. 1939) winner of the **1995 Nobel Prize in Literature**, is celebrated as one of the most popular modern Irish poets. His simply stated, earthy poems, reminiscent of fellow poet W.B. Yeats, make him a true Irish bard. He was born in Mossbawn, County Derry and educated at St. Columbas College, Derry and Queen's University, Belfast. Despite his popularity, he has never forgotten his humble beginnings. His poetry often focuses on the Irish farmland of his youth and the religious prejudices his family suffered as Catholics in Northern Ireland. He has taught at many universities throughout Ireland, England, and the United States. His better known collections of poetry include *Death of a Naturalist* (1966), *Door into the Dark* (1969), *Wintering Out* (1972), *Haw Lantern* (1987), and *Seeing Things* (1991).

Caitlín Maude (1941-1982) was born in Casla, Connemara, County Galway. Through her university studies, she proved herself to be a master at languages. After graduating, she maintained an active role as both teacher and actress. She co-wrote and translated a one-act play with fellow poet Michael Hartnett. Her poetry is published in the collection *Caitlín Maude* (1984).

John F. Deane (b. 1943) was born in Achill, Ireland. He is the founder of *Poetry Ireland* (1979) and has published several collections of poetry. He is now the editor of Dedalus Press as well as a full-time writer.

Augustus Young (b. 1943) (a.k.a. James Hogan) was born in Cork. His work, both poetry and drama, has appeared in magazines throughout England and Ireland. He is currently living and working in London. His poetical works include *Survival* (1969), *On Loaning Hill* (1970) and one translation work called *Dánta Grádha: Love Poems from the Irish* (A.D. 1350-1750) (1975).

Paul Durcan (b. 1944) was born in Dublin and graduated from University College Cork with honors. His style differs from many other modern poets, often referred to as "writings" rather than poetry. His other books include *Jumping the Train Tracks with Angela* (1985), *Berlin Wall Café* (1985), and *Going Home to Russia* (1987).

Gabriel Rosenstock (b. 1949) is the former Chairman of Poetry Ireland/Eigse Eireann. His other credentials include: honorary life member of the Irish Translator's Association and member of both the Society of Irish Playwrights and the Irish Writer's Union. He has authored over 50 books. He has translated into Irish the selected poems of poets such as: Francisco X. Alarcon, Seamus Heaney, and Günter Grass. His own collections include: *Portrait of the Artist as an Abominable Snowman* and *Cold Moon* (1993).

Medbh McGuckian (b. 1950) was born in Belfast and graduated from Queen's University with a B.A. and M.A. in English. She now lives and teaches in Belfast. Her work is published in the following collections: *The Flower Master* (1982), *Venus and the Rain* (1984), and *On Ballycastle Beach* (1988).

Fred Johnston (b. 1951) was born in Belfast and worked as a professional journalist for many years. He has lived in both Algeria and Spain and is now living in Galway. He has received both the Hennessy Literary Award (1972) and an Arts Council Literary Bursary (1988). He is one of the founders of the Irish Writers Co-op and has published three collections of poetry and one novel.

Paul Muldoon (b. 1951) was born in County Armagh and educated at St. Patrick's College, Armagh, and Queen's University, Belfast. He now lives and works in America, often using his Irish experience in his writing. His collections include *New Weather* (1973), *Mules* (1977), and *Selected Poems* (1986).

Gabriel Fitzmaurice (b. 1952) was born in Moyvane, County Kerry. He now lives and teaches in the Local National School. He has published many books in both English and Irish, including many verse translations and ballads. His other works include *An Crann Faoi Bhláth/ The Flowering Tree* (1991) and *The Father's Press* (1992).

Nuala Ní Dhomhnail (b. 1952) is celebrated as one of the prominent Irish women poets of her time. She was born in Lancashire and grew up in the Kerry Gaeltacht. After living abroad in both Holland and Turkey, she settled in Dublin with her husband and children. She is currently writer-in-residence at University College Cork. Many of her Gaelic poems have been translated, by Michael Harnett and herself, in such collections as *Contemporary Irish Poetry* (1988) and *Selected Poems* (1988). Her Gaelic publications include *An Dealg Droighin* (1981) and *Féar Suaithinseach* (1984).

Jo Slade (b. 1952) was born in Berkhamsted, Hertfordshire, England and educated at Limerick and National Colleges of Art. She now works as a painter and poet. Her collections include *In Fields I Hear Them Sing* (1989) and *The Vigilant One.*

Sara Berkeley (b. 1967) was born in Dublin. Her other works include: *Penn* (1986) and *Home Movie Nights* (1989).

Glenda Cimino was born in the United States and moved to Ireland in 1972. In Dublin, she co-founded the once prominent literary publishing house Beaver Row Press (1988). Her first book of poetry, *Cicada*, was published in 1988.

Mary O'Malley was born in Connemara and educated at University College, Galway. She taught English for eight years at the New University of Lisbon, Portugal. She has now moved back to Ireland and lives in Galway. Her first published collection is called: *A Consideration of Silk* (1990).

Peadar Mc Daid, illustrator, is a self-taught artist living and working in his native town of Letterkenny, County Donegal, Ireland. The contents and style of his work are influenced by the Celtic myths and legends of historical, romantic Ireland. For the past five years, he has worked to develop and perfect his own style utilizing the pen and ink medium.